JULIA RIPPY BOONE

BROADMAN PRESS
Nashville, Tennessee

© Copyright 1984 • Broadman Press
All rights reserved.

4211-40
ISBN: 0-8054-1140-2

Dewey Decimal Classification: 220
Subject heading: BIBLE
Library of Congress Catalog Card Number: 81-69259
Printed in the United States of America

Library of Congress Cataloging in Publication Data

Boone, Julia Rippy, 1928-
    Getting to know your Bible.

    Bibliography: p.
    1. Bible—Introductions.   I. Title.
BS475.2.B6   1984   220.6'1   81-69259
ISBN 0-8054-1140-2

Contents

SECTION 1

Introduction

How This Book Can Be Used

This book can be used in several ways. It can be read simply for general information. It can be used as a resource book. It can be used as a day-by-day study guide. And it can be used as a text by groups who want to study the whole Bible or a portion of it.

For those who want general information

This book can serve as a basic introduction to the whole Bible. It is brief, and can be read in a short time, yet it presents an overview of the entire Bible.

For those who want resource material

In addition to the information given in the basic text, there are maps and charts that can be used for study or teaching purposes. The bibliography contains a list of helpful study books plus descriptions telling the kind of information in each. Included also is a list of related topics for the teacher or student who wants ideas for discovering more detail about each section of the Bible.

For those who want a day-by-day study guide

At intervals throughout this book suggestions are given for daily Bible readings. The suggested portions do not cover every word of the Bible but do include many major points and events. They should be read in conjunction with a study of this manual (see Contents page).

For groups wanting a study guide

This book can serve as a text for members of a Bible study group. The Daily Bible Reading suggestions, which cover a one-year period, can be used as weekly or bimonthly divisions.

Between meetings each individual group member should read the assigned portion of the Bible plus a corresponding section of the text. At meetings all members could discuss the Scripture portion, and a leader could add thoughts from some Bible commentaries. In addition one or more members could give reports on some of the topics listed on the same page as the Daily Bible Reading suggestions. Information for such reports can be found in the kind of books listed in the bibliography at the back of this manual.

What This Book Is About

Before a piece of land can be developed into a shopping center or a park or an apartment complex, a survey must be made to determine its size, its high and low points, its lakes and streams. The information gained becomes a tool in the hands of those who want to use the land.

This book is that kind of tool. It is a small sketch of a large work—the Bible.

The Bible is a complex book. Some parts of it can be understood by a small child. Other parts challenge the most learned theologian, for the Bible is, as an ancient sage said, "a stream of running water, where alike the elephant may swim, and the lamb walk without losing its feet."

Most people today who are interested in the Bible at all are somewhat familiar with it. If they have been active in a church, they have heard ministers preach on its great themes of forgiveness, love, hope. They know that it is a Book of and for faith and that the central subject is God. They have learned that the Bible contains sixty-six smaller books, thirty-nine in the Old Testament and twenty-seven in the New. They have become familiar with the names of biblical personalities—Joseph, Moses, David—and with biblical places—Egypt, Jerusalem, the Sea of Galilee. Many know some Scripture by heart—the twenty-third Psalm, John 3:16, the second chapter of Luke. They have studied the life of Jesus and his teachings; they are acquainted with Paul and his letters.

Yet even people who know quite a bit about the Bible can experience surprise at the amount of information it contains. And many who would like to read the Bible straight through from beginning to end find themselves involved in a labor of frustration rather than a labor of love.

The reasons are many. Some of the books follow one another in logical sequence; others do not. The time in which certain events took place seems important, yet few dates are given. Countries and nations mentioned existed long ago and are easily confused because the countries had different names at different times. Speeches made by some of the great personalities of the Bible were designed to meet the needs of the people to whom they were originally addressed, and the modern reader may know little about those people and the circumstances in which they lived.

This manual is designed to help meet those needs. It presents a concise view of the entire Bible, a bare frame, showing how the parts connect to form a whole. It begins at the beginning of the Bible and moves straight through to the end, broadly, not minutely. Timelines and maps are used to make the presentation clearer. In effect, the reader is led to look at the Bible much as one might view a town from a high tower. From the vantage point of a tower, individual homes and buildings could be distinguished, yet each would be seen in relationship to the others.

That is the point of this book. The reader is not to spend an excessive amount of time with each part of the Bible, but one is to aim toward developing relationship keys that make the total picture have meaning.

Chart 1.

Old Testament

Books that deal primarily with one family that became a small nation
- Genesis
- Exodus
- Leviticus
- Numbers
- Deuteronomy
- Joshua
- Judges
- Ruth
- 1 Samuel
- 2 Samuel
- 1 Kings
- 2 Kings
- 1 Chronicles
- 2 Chronicles
- Ezra
- Nehemiah
- Esther

Inspired religious writings of God's people in the Old Testament
- Job
- Psalms
- Proverbs
- Ecclesiastes
- Song of Solomon
- Isaiah
- Jeremiah
- Lamentations
- Ezekiel
- Daniel
- Hosea
- Joel
- Amos
- Obadiah
- Jonah
- Micah
- Nahum
- Habakkuk
- Zephaniah
- Haggai
- Zechariah
- Malachi

New Testament

First four each tell of Jesus Christ who was born among the descendants of the Old Testament family; Acts tells of the churches begun as a result of Christ's resurrection and the gift of the Holy Spirit
- Matthew
- Mark
- Luke
- John
- Acts

Mostly letters written to help the churches told about in Acts
- Romans
- 1 Corinthians
- 2 Corinthians
- Galatians
- Ephesians
- Philippians
- Colossians
- 1 Thessalonians
- 2 Thessalonians
- 1 Timothy
- 2 Timothy
- Titus
- Philemon
- Hebrews
- James
- 1 Peter
- 2 Peter
- 1 John
- 2 John
- 3 John
- Jude
- Revelation

What the Bible Is About

The Bible is the sacred book of the Christian religion, and its main topic is God, yet it is not a manual on the Christian faith, nor does it give detailed facts about God. Instead, it teaches through a variety of ways.

Each of the sixty-six smaller books in the Bible has distinctive characteristics, and none can be described in precisely the same way as any other. Looked at very broadly, however, the books fall logically into four separate divisions, two in the Old Testament and two in the New. (See chart 1.)

The first division consists of the first seventeen Old Testament books, Genesis through Esther. These books deal primarily with one particular family that grew into a nation. The books tell what happened to these people, their kings, their priests, their wars, their religion, their laws. This part of the Bible is written somewhat like a biography. As in a biography only the most memorable happenings are included, not everything. And as in a biography some of the events are good, and some are not.

From these books it is apparent that biblical people, like modern readers of the Bible, were free to choose or reject religious beliefs. Because of their culture, few considered atheism; they were concerned about which god to choose rather than whether to choose a god at all. They made varying decisions based on events, personal experiences, influence of neighbors, the words of religious leaders—the same way people in all cultures have made decisions.

The people told about in these books were real people who belong to the history of the world. They were affected by the same peace, the same wars, the same weather, that affected all others who lived in the same vicinity at the same time. A study of them is, therefore, a study of minds and hearts set against the background of history.

The second group of books in the Old Testament, Job through Malachi, can be classed as inspired religious writings by God's people. The writings include songs, poetry, speeches given by religious leaders, and prophetic writings. They express the emotions of the people who wrote—praise of God, fear of war, anguish over evil behavior, joy over the solution of a problem. The writers were deep thinkers who asked perplexing questions and searched for answers. Often they did not discover the direct answers they sought but something greater—a relationship with God that provided a satisfaction they had not dreamed possible.

The third group of books in the Bible consists of the first five books in the New Testament. The first four of these are four separate accounts of the life of Jesus Christ. Jesus was born among the people who were descendants of those told about in the Old Testament. Therefore, the history in the Old Testament is closely related to the events of the New. The major event in the Bible to Christians is the coming of Christ, and Christ's coming was a divine breakthrough into *history*. Acts, the fifth book in the New Testament, is connected with the first four in that it tells what happened after the events recorded in the first four books.

The fourth group of books in the Bible, the last twenty-two in the New

Testament, are mostly letters written by or to people told about in Acts. All the writings are directed toward early churches or to individuals who were involved in the early churches.

The "canon" of the Bible, that is the standard list of books accepted as Scripture, are books that have been approved in two ways. First, they are books that rose to the position of Scripture through their influence and use. They became Scripture without any council meeting or any group voting that they were of Scripture quality. Second, the list received official approval at council meetings by religious leaders who voted on an official list. Those books approved at the meetings were ones that had already come into use.

The Old Testament must have been accepted as Scripture according to its three divisions. By 400 BC the Law (the first five books sometimes called Torah) was accepted as Scripture. By 200 BC the prophetic writings were accepted as Scripture. Most believe that the books that make up the Writings were basically accepted as Scripture at the Council of Jamnia about AD 90. Generally speaking, the Old Testament, as we know it, was all accepted as Scripture by around AD 100.[1]

The first person to list the accepted books of the New Testament to be the twenty-seven accepted today was Athanasius of Alexander in his Easter Letter of 367. However, some books were still not accepted by some parts of Christianity. Usually AD 400 is the accepted date for the New Testament canon being basically finished.[2]

When Biblical Events Took Place

The events told about in the Old Testament covered a long period of time. The events told about in the New Testament covered only about as many years as an ordinary lifetime. (See chart 2.)

Although completely accurate dating of many biblical events is not possible, the approximate time of major happenings will be shown on a timeline at various intervals throughout this book. The timelines use the BC-AD system of dating common in most countries today.

The BC-AD system grew out of an idea developed about 1500 years ago by a monk named Dionysius. Dionysius was assigned the task of filing important Christian papers—records of church council meetings and other documents—that had been accumulating over a long period of time. He decided to file them according to how much time had passed between the birth of Christ and the writing of the paper. Documents written 325 years after the birth of Christ received the date 325; ones written 410 years after the birth of Christ received the date 410, and so on. Dionysius made a slight mistake in his calculations; Christ was actually born

Chart 2.
When events in the Bible took place.

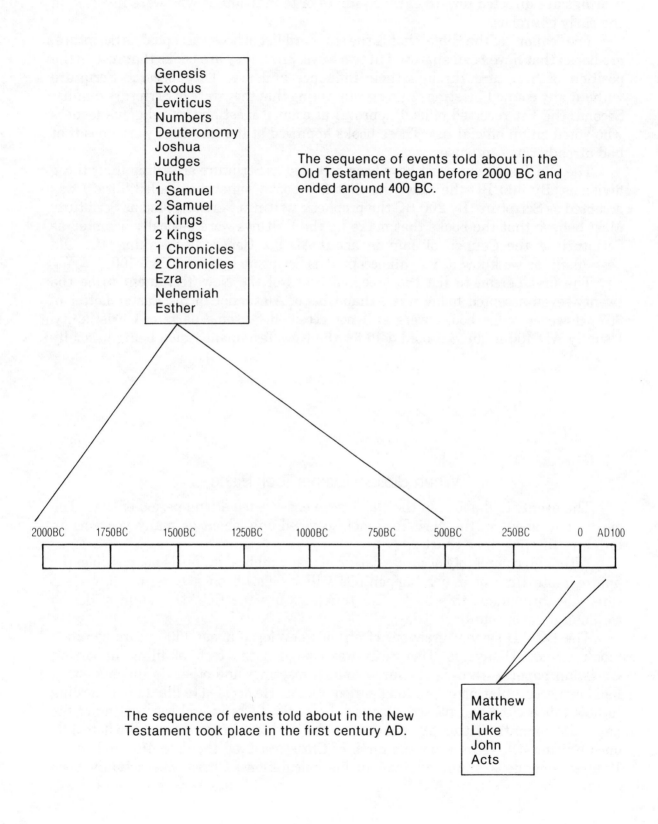

Genesis
Exodus
Leviticus
Numbers
Deuteronomy
Joshua
Judges
Ruth
1 Samuel
2 Samuel
1 Kings
2 Kings
1 Chronicles
2 Chronicles
Ezra
Nehemiah
Esther

The sequence of events told about in the Old Testament began before 2000 BC and ended around 400 BC.

| 2000BC | 1750BC | 1500BC | 1250BC | 1000BC | 750BC | 500BC | 250BC | 0 | AD100 |

The sequence of events told about in the New Testament took place in the first century AD.

Matthew
Mark
Luke
John
Acts

several years earlier than Dionysius figured. Still his measurements, without correction, were gradually adopted by all Christians and became the basis for the Christian calendar. Years before Christ's birth began to be spoken of as BC (before Christ) years. Years after Christ's birth began to be spoken of as AD years (*anno Domini,* Latin for "in the year of the Lord" but used as though it means after Christ years).

When the events in the Bible took place is, of course, not identical with when the information about them was written down. The writing was done by individuals who were moved by God's Spirit to record the words that earlier had only been spoken. The names of many of these people are mentioned in the Bible although others are not known. The priests had much to do with the writing of the Old Testament, particularly the sections that have to do with worship. Parts of the Old Testament were probably recorded as early as 1800 BC, and the writing continued through about 200 BC. Most of the New Testament was written in less than fifty years, probably within the time segment between AD 50 and AD 100.

Where Biblical Events Took Place

The events told about in both the Old and New Testaments took place in the land surrounding the eastern half of the Mediterranean Sea. (See chart 3.) As the years passed, the boundaries of countries in that area constantly shifted because of wars and changes in government. Cities and lakes were renamed in honor of new rulers. And names that weren't changed sometimes began to be pronounced and spelled differently because of the influence of foreign languages.

Because such changes are so much a part of the biblical record, it is difficult to study the Bible without frequent references to maps. For that reason maps are located at intervals throughout this book. Each map reflects the most decisive changes that took place in the particular part of the Bible that is being discussed.

---

[1]*The Broadman Bible Commentary,* Vol. 1, revised, Clifton J. Allen, ed. (Nashville: Broadman Press, 1973), pp. 50-52.
[2]*The Broadman Bible Commentary,* Vol. 8, Clifton J. Allen, ed. (Nashville: Broadman Press, 1969), pp. 20-21.

Chart 3.

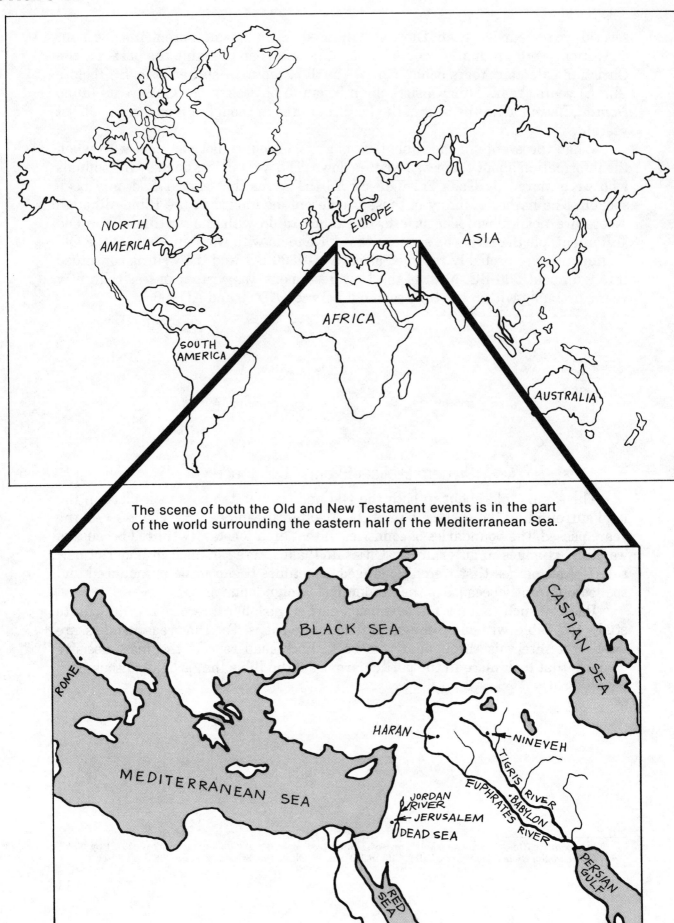

The scene of both the Old and New Testament events is in the part of the world surrounding the eastern half of the Mediterranean Sea.

SECTION 2
The First Seventeen Books of the Bible

Basic to Bible study is a familiarity with the account that is given in the first seventeen books of the Old Testament. An acquaintance with it is as essential for the Bible student as knowing the alphabet is to one who wishes to use a dictionary or as knowing how to count is to one who wishes to add and subtract numbers.

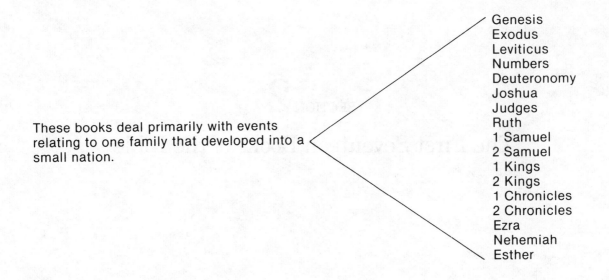

These books deal primarily with events relating to one family that developed into a small nation.

Genesis
Exodus
Leviticus
Numbers
Deuteronomy
Joshua
Judges
Ruth
1 Samuel
2 Samuel
1 Kings
2 Kings
1 Chronicles
2 Chronicles
Ezra
Nehemiah
Esther

The following pages contain brief sketches of those first seventeen Old Testament books. Because the history covered in the books involves so many changes in location, the books are divided into groups according to the unity they bear to one another. A map and timeline precedes each group, and a memory jog page follows each.

Chart 4.
Genesis Through Deuteronomy

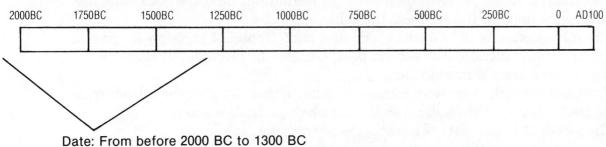

2000BC	1750BC	1500BC	1250BC	1000BC	750BC	500BC	250BC	0	AD100

Date: From before 2000 BC to 1300 BC

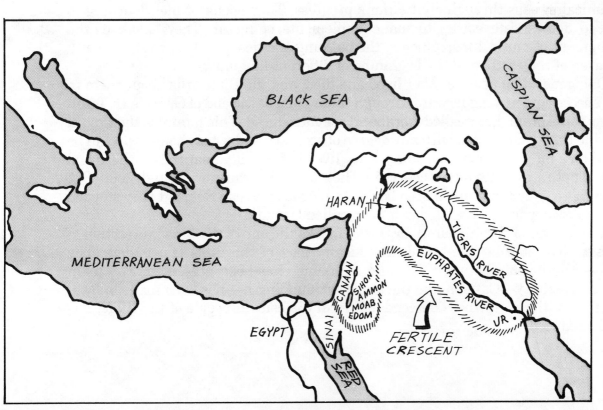

Genesis

The Hebrew name for Genesis means "in beginning," and the book tells just what the name implies. It introduces the Bible.

The introduction is in two parts. The first part, Genesis 1 through 11, gives a broad overall introduction. The second part, Genesis 12 through 50, narrows the view and gives a specific introduction.

Genesis 1 through 11 serves a purpose similar to that found in the introduction of most books. It gives the reader insight into what the book is about.

The accounts in this part of Genesis are universal in scope.

> Creation (Gen. 1—2)
> Adam and Eve and their children (Gen. 3—4)
> Noah and a great flood (Gen. 6—10)
> The tower of Babel (Gen. 11:1–9)

They open like a hymn, strumming chords beyond human understanding, yet speaking of what all people wonder about—of God who created all things and his relationship to that which he had created. As these chapters speak of the beginning of the heavens and the earth, they provide for the reader, not information about the how of creation, but the scene of the Bible—the everyday world of light and darkness, of land and water, of plants and animals. As they speak of people they show the human traits that have been common in all generations—pride, jealousy, anger—and the behavior, the *sins*, that result when these traits are uncontrolled. It also shows faith, love, and loyalty on the part of some people. As they speak of God they show that this Book, this Bible, is not simply a book of history or facts or even story. It is about the ultimate meaning of human life. It is about God's concern for people; it is about people's encounters with the living God.

The accounts in these first eleven chapters begin in antiquity and move with rhythmical sweeps through civilization's progress. They speak of men learning to farm, to domesticate cattle, to make implements of metal. They speak of the development of musical instruments, the building of cities, people spreading over a wide area of the earth, and the beginning of different languages.

One generation after another lived and died, and the Bible tells about them in rapid succession, moving forward through time. Then at the end of Genesis 11, Terah and his son Abram (later called Abraham) are introduced. This family is the first in the Bible that can be dated with any degree of accuracy and whose hometown can be located on a map with some certainty. They lived in Ur, a city near the southern end of the Euphrates River. (See chart 5.) They left Ur, probably around 2000 BC, intending to go to Canaan, an area beside the Mediterranean Sea; but they stopped at the halfway point and settled in a town called Haran.

The arrival of Terah's family in Haran marks the end of the prologue section of Genesis. At that point the broad introductory part of the Bible is complete. The theme—relationship between God and mankind—has been presented. The main theater of activity—Canaan and the lands surrounding it—has been made known. And Abram, the man whose descendants form the central people of the Bible, has been introduced.

Chart 5.
Mesopotamia, the Fertile Crescent, and Ur

The area between the Tigris and Euphrates rivers is known as a cradle of civilization. In ancient times it was often called Mesopotamia, a word meaning "between the rivers."

In Mesopotamia, between the Tigris and Euphrates and arching from them toward the Mediterranean Sea, is an area once known as the Fertile Crescent. It was a long curve that stretched like a green rainbow across the desert. Travelers followed this curve when going from Egypt to Mesopotamia because along it water and food could be obtained. Abraham must have followed the route of the crescent when he traveled from Ur to Haran.

Ur, Abraham's original home, was at the southern end of the crescent beside the Euphrates River. At the time of Abraham, Ur was probably one of the world's leading cities. Today it has been partially excavated by archaeologists. Among the ruins are two-story brick houses with patios; one still contains remains of an indoor plumbing system. Articles found in the city include a solid gold helmet set with jewels, business records, hymns, facial makeup. The people of Ur wrote in the cuneiform script named for the cuneus (wedge) shaped end of the writing stick used to make indentions in soft clay tablets. Their mathematical system, based on twelve, gave the modern world the custom of placing twelve hours in a day and of putting 360 degrees in a circle.

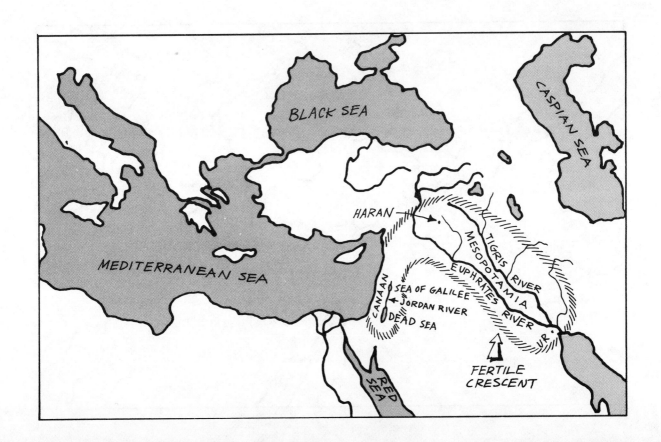

Chart 6.
Cross Section of Canaan

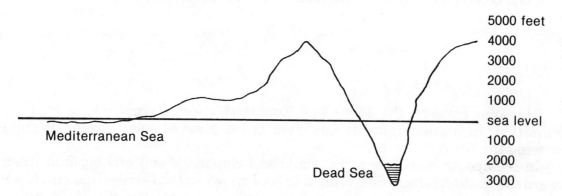

The land once known as Canaan has more surface variations for its size than any comparable area in the world. An earth fault—a giant crack—forms a crevice through the center. In this crevice lie the Sea of Galilee, the Jordan River, and the lowest spot on earth, the Dead Sea. The same fault, known as the Great Rift, extends under the Red Sea and thrusts into Africa, ending near the equator where mountain lakes and snows give birth to the mighty Nile.

Canaan's topography creates extreme variations in climate; much of the land is barren because of inadequate water supplies. Yet, Canaan, in biblical times, had an asset no other area had: location. It connected Asia to Africa. All trade between the two continents had to cross Canaan; there was no other bridge. Ambitious kings in ancient times vied for control of Canaan for who controlled Canaan controlled the world's most heavily traveled routes. By charging a toll for the use of the route the owner was assured of a rich revenue.

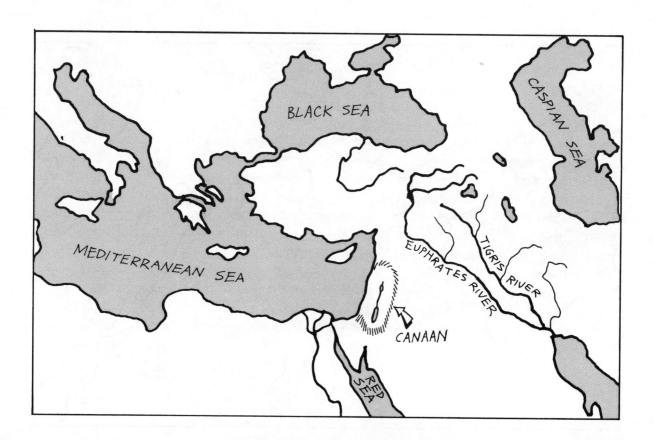

The second section of Genesis, chapters 12 through 50, moves through time at a much slower pace than the first section. Instead of taking giant leaps over broad centuries, it covers only four generations of a principal biblical family. By focusing upon one family, the Bible record shifts from a universal setting among all people to a particular setting among a select group. Yet the particular has universal applications.

The account begins with Abram, Terah's son, who was told by God to leave his father's home and go "to the land that I will show you" (Gen. 12:1). Taking with him his wife Sarai and his nephew Lot, Abram went to Canaan. (See chart 6.) In Canaan, God spoke to Abram again, telling him that his descendants would some-day own the land he had just entered.

Those words introduce two key elements that are important throughout the entire Bible: Canaan became the Promised Land, and Abraham's descendants became the Chosen People. Yet, the words were puzzling to Abram because he had no descendants, and his wife was too old to have children. He considered adopting one of his slaves as his heir, a common practice in that day. But Sarai persuaded him to try another common practice—to have a child by her maid Hagar. A child was born to Hagar, the maid, and was named Ishmael. (Modern Arabs claim kinship to Abraham through Ishmael.) Later, however, Sarah, despite her age, gave birth to a son. The child, named Isaac, became Abraham's principal heir. Isaac was not only the child of Abraham's wife but the child of promise born miraculously to a woman past childbearing age. (Jews trace their descent from Abraham through Isaac.)

Isaac had twin sons, Esau and Jacob. Esau's chief contribution to the overall history is that he founded Edom, a country important in both the Old and New Testaments. (In the New Testament, Edom is called by its Greek equivalent, Idumea.) Jacob, the younger of the two sons, is much more prominent in the Bible than Esau; it is through him that the record of the family continued. His twelve sons fathered the principal people in the Bible, the Israelites.

The Israelites were named for Jacob who was also called Israel, a word meaning "he who strives with God." (See Gen. 32:22-32.) Jacob and his twelve sons were living in Canaan when the older sons became jealous of their younger brother Joseph and sold him as a slave. Joseph was taken to Egypt where, after going through some very difficult experiences, he gained a prominent position in the Egyptian government. (At the time a people called Hyksos were ruling Egypt. They had come from the same location as Joseph's ancestors—the eastern Fertile Crescent area. They had invaded Egypt and successfully defeated the country because they had the most modern equipment of the day, a horse-drawn chariot. Egyptians had used the wheel for making pottery, but they had not built a wheeled vehicle for travel or fighting.) While holding his prestigious position, Joseph moved his father and his brothers and their families to Egypt. They began living in the Nile delta where they received royal treatment because of Joseph's official status.

Although Jacob was willing to move to Egypt, he did not want his family to stay there permanently. Canaan was their Promised Land; he wanted his sons to return there, to develop a country, to divide it among themselves, and to set up a government. He spoke of the future, saying that his descendants would return to

Canaan and that a king would come from the family of Judah, his fourthborn son. And the sons of Joseph, Ephraim and Manasseh, were to hold the same rank as their uncles. They were to share in the division of the land as though they had been born to Jacob himself and were his sons, not his grandsons.

Later in the biblical record, when the Israelites returned to Canaan, the land was divided into twelve parts. Ten parts were named for ten of Jacob's sons. No part was named for Joseph, but two parts were named for his sons, Ephraim and Manasseh. No part was named for Levi, the thirdborn son, because that family became the priestly family and therefore lived among all the people rather than in one designated area. The division of Joseph's family into two parts caused the family groups to number thirteen rather than twelve. But because of the Levites' special role as priests they were never counted with the others. The thirteen groups, commonly called tribes, were known as "the twelve tribes of Israel."

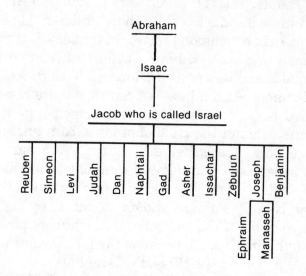

When Jacob died, his body was taken back to Canaan for burial, but his sons returned to Egypt. Genesis concludes with the twelve families living in Egypt, an ending that completes the introduction of the Bible. The twelve sons form the nucleus of a people who will be followed through fifteen centuries as the rest of the biblical account unfolds.

Exodus

Exodus, named for the exit of the Israelites from Egypt, is closely linked to Genesis, although several centuries elapsed between the two books. During those centuries two changes took place that decidedly affected the future of the descendants of Jacob.

One: the twelve families grew substantially in number. Since they did not intermarry with Egyptians, they became a distinct group of people. In Exodus they are spoken of as Israelites because they were descendants of Israel (Jacob) and also as Hebrews, a name thought to be equivalent to the word *Habiru* which means "outsiders." (Habiru was a broad term used to refer to the many seminomadic groups

20

who lived in and around the Fertile Crescent area. It described their style of life more than their race. The word *Hebrew* gradually became more specific, referring both to the descendants of Jacob and to their language.)

Two: the Egyptian government changed. A new ruler came to the throne, one who viewed the Israelites quite differently from the way the king during Joseph's lifetime had viewed them. He saw Joseph's relatives, not as friends of the king, but as dangerous foreigners—a subversive group that might join an enemy against Egypt if Egypt were attacked. To prevent such a possibility the king (Pharaoh) ordered guards over the Israelites. Joseph's kin suddenly found themselves with a new and unwelcome status; they had been reduced from prominent guests to slaves.

As long as life had gone well for the Israelites they had made no attempt to leave Egypt. Stories had been handed down to them about the God of their ancestors who had spoken to Abraham and who had designated Canaan as the Promised Land of his descendants. But they had not felt stimulated to go there; they saw no reason to leave the comforts of Egypt. Slavery, however, caused new thoughts to enter their heads. They cried out to God, and God responded to their groanings.

Exodus records the difficulties the Israelites endured as slaves. It records the dramatic happenings that led to their escaping from Egypt. And it records the events that took place during the first year that they were away from Egypt.

Faith is at the heart of the book—not a mystical faith, but a relationship with the God who takes part in human affairs. He is the God who makes himself known through his actions, the God who gives good to human beings, but who expects them to reflect the same kind of goodness.

Moses, a remarkable and deeply spiritual man, is the principal character in the book. He stimulated the Israelites to develop faith in the God who cared enough about them to dramatically end the degrading situation they had been forced into. He became their leader both in the successful, though precarious, escape from Egypt, and during the traumatic years that followed.

The actual Exodus from Egypt is the foremost event in the book, and to the nation produced by that occurrence, the crucial experience of the entire Old Testament. It marked the historical beginning of the Israelites as a separate people, a beginning not associated with an organizing team, but with a miraculous event. The passing from bondage to freedom was not just an escape from armed guards. It was a sign that God *is* and that he intervenes in the affairs of people. It was light—not like a blinding flash in the sky but a clearly visible act that would not have taken place without divine power affecting a human situation.

The Exodus became *the central occasion* in Israel's memory. It was the pivotal point in their existence. Just as people remember, not their births but the events that give meaning to their lives, so the Israelites recalled the Exodus as the experience that set their destiny, their vocation, their purpose. It changed them from an obscure people to a people who would affect the course of history.

Besides the Exodus, the other major developments in the Book of Exodus are three. First, a yearly festival, Passover, was begun to commemorate the night of the Exodus. Second, laws that came to be known as the Ten Commandments were given. And third, a portable religious center—the tabernacle—was constructed, and the tribe of Levi was named as caretakers of it and as religious instructors for the people.

The Passover festival was begun in memory of the last of ten plagues that struck the Egyptians in rapid succession but did not touch the Israelites. The tenth plague, the death of the firstborn in every Egyptian household, struck on the night the Israelites left Egypt. Because the plague did not strike the Israelites, but passed over, the festival commemorating the miracle was given the name Passover.

The Passover celebration is the reliving of the *event* of the Exodus. The Passover festival is entered into as a participant in the long ago; the past is brought to the present, and Passover becomes what the Lord did for *me*.

Today Passover is the most memorable of all Jewish holidays. It is observed at the time of the spring equinox and always includes the eating of a special meal called the seder. Foods served remind the people of the years of Egyptian slavery. A blend of nuts and apples resembles mortar used in the building projects the slaves were forced to work on. Bitter herbs bring to mind the bitter slave life. Unleavened bread reminds participants that no yeast was in the bread the Israelites took from Egypt. (Modern Jewish children make a game of searching their homes for yeast just before Passover.)

After leaving Egypt, the Israelites traveled southeast (rather than north where they would have had to pass forts) and after several weeks reached Mount Sinai. There, at their first meeting as free, independent people, they accepted the Ten Commandments as their basic set of laws.

With the adoption of the Ten Commandments the Israelites entered into a covenant with God. At that time there were two types of covenants in common use. One, a parity covenant, was made between equal parties who each assumed a balanced portion of an agreement. The other, a suzerainty covenant, was between unequals as between a king and a subject. The king's part was largely one of giving, the subject's one of receiving.

The covenant between the Israelites and God was an agreement between one with power and another with need. It was between one who had graciously brought the Israelites out of bondage and who wanted to continue caring for them, and those who had received this kindness and needed continued care. The covenant was a pledge from God that he would watch over and protect the Israelites if they would obey his commandments. It was a pledge from the Israelites that they would obey God's commandments if he would watch over and protect them.

The Ten Commandments, plus other laws given in the first five books of the Old Testament, began to be spoken of as "the Law." The rest of the Bible is intimately entwined with the Law—the interpretations of it, the obeying of it, the disobeying of it, and the consequences of obeying or disobeying.

The Exodus and the covenant of Sinai made the people of Israel a community of faith. It caused them to record their history not as history in the usual sense but with a divine dimension. Biblical history is sacred history. It tells of the mighty acts of God whereby he makes himself known, of God who is not aloof from human affairs but takes part in them. The acts recorded are not indisputable proofs of God, rather they are signs of God's presence. Signs and wonders are given that people may know who really runs history. They are evidences of God who is accepted in faith and trust.

In memory of the day the Ten Commandments were given, a second annual holiday was established—Pentecost. (Though a religious rather than a national holiday, Pentecost holds some similarity to America's Independence Day. It was the day the Israelites recognized their unity as one people.) The name *Pentecost*, which means fifty, was given to the holiday because it is commemorated on the fiftieth day after Passover. The festival is also known as the Feast of the Weeks because fifty days includes a week of weeks—seven days times seven weeks. Several other titles are associated with it, among them Festival of the Giving of the Law, Feast of Harvest, and Day of Firstfruits. Gifts of firstfruits of the orchard and garden were customarily given to priests during the holiday. The celebration takes place in early summer just as the first crops are ripening.

To Passover and Pentecost a third annual holiday was added, a harvest festival held at the fall equinox. Given the name Feast of Tabernacles (*tabernacle* means test), the holiday was to remind the Israelites of the difficult living conditions the escaped slaves endured in the desert. It is also called the Feast of the Booths. Families in later biblical times celebrated the holiday by living in rustic branch arbors, or booths, during the festival week. Modern celebrants sometimes prop a cardboard lean-to against a building, or construct a temporary picnic shelter in their backyard. (Jewish children enjoy decorating the booths with fruits and vegetables much as Christian children enjoy decorating Christmas trees.) Others

today symbolize shelters by putting greenery over a front door, or by attaching flowers to a light fixture hanging over a dining table.

About half the Book of Exodus is concerned with the plan and construction of the portable religious center called the tabernacle. Gifts for its construction came from people "of a generous heart" (35:5); no one was compelled to give. The building symbolized the fact that the Israelites were a theocracy; they had no king but recognized God as their supreme ruler. The appointment of the Levites as the religious leaders meant that the priesthood would be hereditary. They were to care for the tabernacle, preside over the religious festivals, and act as instructors and interpreters of the laws given by God.

Leviticus

Leviticus, named for the Levites, is a manual of religious ceremonies. It offered guidelines for worshiping God by priests and people. Exodus ends with the completion of the tabernacle as a place of worship; Leviticus contains ceremonies and laws used in connection with worship. In addition to spiritual matters, the laws given in Leviticus also concern cleanliness (of body, food, and dwellings), the diagnosing of illnesses, quarantines to prevent the spread of contagious diseases, the kind of restitution that should be made when a person or animal damages something belonging to another.

The ceremonies in Leviticus are outward acts, as bowing the head in prayer is an outward act, but represent an inward experience. A principal act mentioned in Leviticus is that of sacrifice. A sacrifice was the offering of a gift of cereal or an animal to God. Sometimes a sacrifice was burned as a "whole offering"; often only the inedible portions were burned with some of the best portions given to the priests and the rest eaten by worshipers at a meal of dedication or thanksgiving. The gifts were not given because the people believed that God consumed what was burned or that he needed food. Gifts were brought to represent restoring a relationship with God that had been broken because of sin, or they were brought in recognition of what God had provided.

The most important religious ceremony mentioned in Leviticus is the Day of Atonement, the holiest day of the Israelite year. The day was set aside as a day of cleansing for the whole nation, including the priests. It was a time for everyone to repent of sins committed during the past year, and of beginning anew. As described in Leviticus 16, on the Day of Atonement all sins from the past were figuratively laid on two animals. One animal was sacrificed and burned, symbolically destroying the sins laid on him. The other was released in the desert, symbolically sending the sins so far away they could never return. (The term *scapegoat* arose from the practice of placing sins on a goat and releasing it to wander in the desert.)

The Day of Atonement, presently called Yom Kippur, is still the holiest day of the Jewish year. More Jews attend synagogues on that day than any other in the annual cycle. The services are solemn with no semblance of gaiety. Centuries ago the holiday was both a time of mourning and a time of joy—mourning for the sins of the community and joy at the end of the day because it was a time of new beginning.

The Day of Atonement represents an ever-recurring need for cleansing and repentance. Hebrews 9, in the New Testament, shows that the sacrifice of Christ provided a one-time cleansing that did away with the need of an annual atonement.

The last third of Leviticus, chapters 17—27, is frequently called the "Holiness Code." The word *holy* refers to God's perfect righteousness. Holy people are to reflect that righteousness. The purpose of the Holiness Code is to show the people of a holy God the way to righteous living. This section speaks less about ritual and ceremony and more about high morals and concern for others. It includes the royal law, "Thou shalt love thy neighbour as thyself" (Lev. 19:18).

Numbers

Numbers is named for a census the Israelites took of all the persons who had left Egypt. The main part of the book, however, begins where Exodus ends and gives an account of the next thirty-eight years. (In the Hebrew Scriptures the book is called "In the Wilderness," a title that fits the whole book better than "Numbers.")

The Book of Numbers records information about the life and emotions of the Israelites in their desert environment—the way they arranged their camp, their schedule of travel, the good and bad things that happened, and the belligerent attitudes most of them showed as they faced day-to-day problems. The principal event in the book revolves around reports given by twelve Israelites who were sent to gather information about Canaan.

The twelve men went to Canaan, spent more than a month traveling about, then returned to the Israelite camp with two decidedly different reports. Two of the men—Joshua and Caleb—said the land was ideal, and they should all begin moving there at once. The other ten agreed that the country was most appealing but said the Israelites could never hope to live there. The land was occupied by giants.

Pandemonium broke out. In wild hysteria the people turned back to the nomadic life they hated, refusing to listen to the appeals of Joshua and Caleb. They lacked both faith and emotional stamina and accepted a life they felt able to cope with. For the next forty years the tribes wandered, moving from one temporary campsite to another. During that time all adults who had been twenty or older, except Joshua, Caleb, and Moses, died. (See Num. 14:29-35.) A new generation grew up, a generation not afraid to make plans for settling in Canaan.

Moses, by then an old man and realizing his years of leadership were drawing to a close, appointed Joshua as his successor. The two men worked together as the tribes migrated into the countries on the eastern side of the Jordan River. Plans were made for settling the tribes when they reached Canaan. Two and one-half tribes requested that they be allowed to settle on the eastern side of the Jordan; the other nine and one-half tribes planned to establish homes on the western side.

Deuteronomy

Deuteronomy means "second law." Like Leviticus, Deuteronomy is primarily a book of laws, but they are for the laity, not the priests. The laws largely repeat many of those given in Exodus and Leviticus although others are added. Most of them are presented through speeches that Moses gave near the end of his life.

The book opens on the first day of the fortieth year after the Exodus. Only Moses, Joshua, and Caleb remained alive from those who had been twenty years old or older when they left Egypt. The new generation that had grown up in the wilderness had reached Moab, a small country east of the Jordan River. (Moab had been founded by the son of Lot, Abraham's nephew. See Genesis 19:37, and map, chart 4.) From there they intended to cross the Jordan, move into Canaan, and end their years as wanderers.

Moses was concerned that the new generation be properly prepared for the experiences that were facing them so he called them together and taught them. His speeches fall into four sections.

Deuteronomy 1 through 3 gives a review of the forty years that had passed since the Israelites left Egypt. It speaks of where they had traveled, the care God gave them, the blessings they had when they obeyed God, and the difficulties they endured when they rebelled.

Section two, Deuteronomy 4 through 28, opens with a plea for the Israelites to recall their history, teach it to their children, and profit from the lessons it taught. Moses then reviewed the laws that had been given at Mount Sinai, beginning with the Ten Commandments (Deut. 5) and from there moving into a broad spectrum of laws to help them as they settled in new communities. As he spoke, Moses showed that God gave laws, not as a burden to be borne but as directions for living the good life. The laws touch a vast array of subjects from keeping an army camp clean to knowing when to charge interest on a loan. The laws emphasize compassion—Moses often repeated the phrase, "Remember that you were a servant" (5:15). They emphasize generosity—tithing, leaving some produce in the fields for strangers. They emphasize keeping instructive information before their eyes—observing Passover, Pentecost, Tabernacles and teaching the children why; having the king (when the time came for a king) own a copy of the law and "read in it all the days of his life" (17:19).

This section forms the nucleus of the book and includes a ceremony the Israelites were told to perform after they settled in Canaan. They were to gather at Mount Ebal and Mount Gerizim, two mountains opposite each other near the center of the country (Deut. 27:4-13). (The area is important throughout the Bible. It was in that vicinity that God spoke to Abraham, promising him the land as a possession. Jacob bought land there; Joseph's bones were buried there; Joshua gave an important address there; and the city of Shechem, important in the Book of 1 Kings, was near there. The New Testament Book of John, chapter 4, tells of Jesus talking with a woman near there, and the woman mentioned that her ancestors had worshiped on those mountains.) Between the two mountains the people were to set up stones and write on them the laws Moses had taught. Then they were to stand on the mountains, six tribes on each, and speak back and forth to each other, one group saying blessings that would come if they followed God's laws, the other cursings that would come if they did not (Deut. 27:14 to 28: 1-6).

In the third portion of Deuteronomy, chapters 29 and 30, Moses asked the new generation to renew the covenant with God that their fathers had made. He emphasized the blessings that would come through serving God, saying that the commands were not too hard. Keeping them was the way to life and happiness; not keeping them was the way to defeat and misery.

The final portion of the book, chapters 31 through 34, contains Moses' final charges to the Israelites and his commissioning of Joshua as his successor (Deut. 31:7-8). The book ends with the death of Moses. He died on Mount Nebo in Moab (Deut. 34:1-6), an elevation that provided for the great leader a panoramic view of the land he had been leading the Israelites toward for so many years.

To many modern Jews the most valuable of all Scriptures is found in Deuteronomy 6:4-9: "Hear, O Israel: The Lord our God is one Lord; and you shall love the Lord your God with all your heart, and with all your soul, and with all your might. And these words which I command you this day shall be upon your heart; and you shall teach them diligently to your children, and shall talk of them when you sit in your house, and when you walk by the way, and when you lie down, and when you rise. And you shall bind them as a sign upon your hand, and they shall be frontlets between your eyes. And you shall write them on the doorposts of your house and on your gates."

In obedience to the command, many Jewish families attach a small case called a mezzuzah to the door frames of their homes. The case contains the above Scripture, or some other almost identical. (Compare Deut. 11:1-21.) In addition some devout Jews carry the command further by wearing, during hours of prayer, small leather cube-shaped cases containing Scripture. One box is bound to the forehead as a "frontlet" between the eyes; another is tied to the left hand.

The New Testament makes much use of Deuteronomy. When Jesus was asked, "Which commandment is the first of all?" (Mark 12:28), he answered, "The first is, 'Hear, O Israel: The Lord our God, the Lord is one; and you shall love the Lord your God with all your heart, and with all your soul, and with all your mind, and with all your strength'" (Mark 12:29-39).

Daily Bible Reading Schedule

Week 1
Gen. 1
Gen. 2
Gen. 3
Gen. 4
Gen. 6:9-14; 7:1-10,17-24; 8:13-17
Gen. 11:1-9,24-32
Gen. 12:1-7; 15:1-5; 16:1-3,15; 21:1-3

Week 2
Gen. 25:19-27; 28:1-5; 35:22b-26
Gen. 37:1-4,23-28; 41:1-13
Gen. 41:14-40
Gen. 42:6; 47:5-6,27 to 48:6
Gen. 50:15-26
Ex. 1:1-14
Ex. 1:15 to 2:10

Week 3
Ex. 2:11-25
Ex. 3:1-20
Ex. 11:10 to 12:42
Ex. 13:17-19; 14:5-14,21-30
Ex. 15:22-27
Ex. 16:1-5,14-31
Ex. 19:1-9; 20:1-20

Week 4
Ex. 25:1-9; 28:1-4
Ex. 40:16-38
Lev. 19:9-18
Num. 1:1-4,49; 13:1-3,17-20
Num. 13:25 to 14:10,26-38
Num. 32:1-29
Num. 33:50 to 34:13

Week 5
Deut. 1:1-3; 5:1-22
Deut. 6:1-15
Deut. 8:1-10
Deut. 8:17 to 9:5
Deut. 27:1-26
Deut. 28:1-19
Deut. 32:45-47; 34:1-12

Suggested Topics for Further Research

Ancient Egypt: land of the pharaohs and pyramids

Ark of the Covenant: a chest, the most sacred object of the tabernacle

Fertile Crescent: the watered curve of land stretching through the desert from the Persian Gulf to the Mediterranean

Hammurabi: Mesopotamian king famous for his code of laws

Hyksos: people who invaded Egypt about 1720 BC and ruled 200 years

Mesopotamia: area between the Tigris and Euphrates rivers

Saint Catherine's Monastery: monastery built where it is believed Moses saw the burning bush

Sumer: an ancient civilization in the Mesopotamian region

Tabernacle: worship center of the early Israelites

Tell: an archaeological term designating a flat-topped hill made by successive cities being built on the same site

Tutankhamen: king of Egypt shortly before the time of Moses; treasures from his tomb have been shown around the world

Ur: probable birthplace of Abraham

Way of the Sea and King's Highway: major roads through Canaan

Ziggurat: pyramid-shaped tower used for worship

Reinforce Your Memory

Genesis _____ the Bible. Genesis 1—11 tells of the beginning of all things; Genesis 12—50 focuses upon the family of _____ through whose descendants the principal people of the Bible, the _____, came into being. At the end of Genesis the fourth generation of that family had settled in _____.

Exodus, named for the _____ of the Israelites from Egypt, begins several _____ after the close of Genesis. A new king had made _____ of the Israelites, and Exodus tells how they gained _____. It also tells of their receiving the _____ _____ as laws, and of the construction of the _____ as a place of worship.

Leviticus is primarily a book of _____.

Numbers, named for a _____ the Israelites took after leaving Egypt, tells of years the Israelites lived as _____ because they were afraid to go to Canaan when they had the chance.

Deuteronomy means _____ _____. The book is chiefly made up of _____ given by _____ who wanted a new generation to learn God's _____.

Draw a timeline showing the probable date of Abraham and of the Exodus.

In the space below draw a map showing Canaan, Egypt, the Sinai Peninsula and the cities of Ur and Haran.

Chart 7.
Joshua, Judges, Ruth

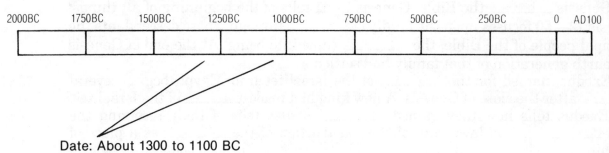

2000BC | 1750BC | 1500BC | 1250BC | 1000BC | 750BC | 500BC | 250BC | 0 | AD100

Date: About 1300 to 1100 BC

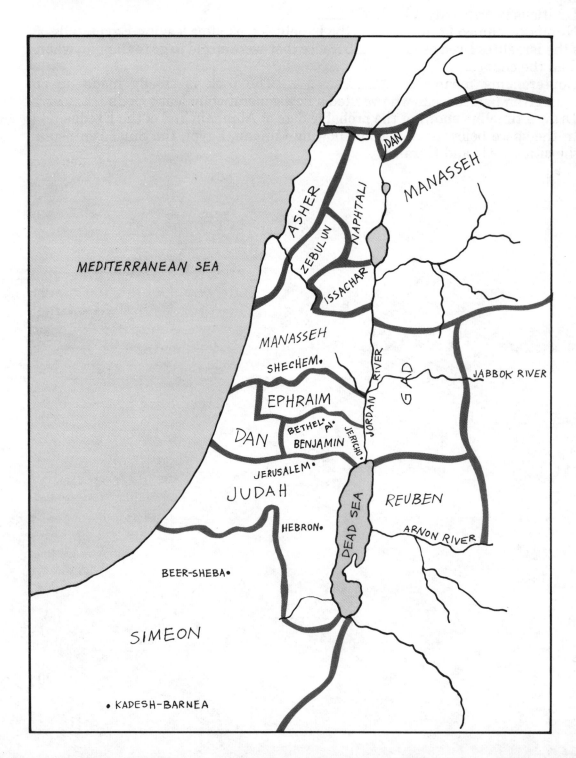

Joshua

The Book of Joshua, named for the foremost person in the book, opens just after the death of Moses, probably around 1250 BC, and covers the entire period of Joshua's leadership. Under Joshua the Israelites entered Canaan and claimed the land as their own. (To a degree Joshua's life is similar to that of America's George Washington. As young men both were sent out to survey the land they would later rule. Each became head of the army, and each served as the first leader of his country.)

The book has three separate sections. The first tells about the conquest of the land. The second shows how the land was divided among the tribes. And the third contains addresses Joshua made to the people.

The conquest of Canaan (chapters 1—12) was made in a series of swift campaigns. The tribes entered the central part of the country by crossing the Jordan River from Moab. (Their crossing of the Jordan while it was in flood stage is one of the outstanding descriptions in the book. The river stopped flowing when the priests carrying the ark of the covenant stepped into the water. When the Canaanites "heard that the Lord had dried up the waters of the Jordan for the people of Israel to cross over, their heart melted, and there was no longer any spirit in them" (Josh. 5:1). The Israelites took Jericho and other cities in central Canaan, then swept into the hills of the south and later made similar thrusts into the north. The rapid campaigns accomplished not only the goal of getting the Israelites into Canaan but of spreading them throughout the land. The conquests described, however, were only initial wedges into the country. The actual settlement, as seen in the rest of the Book of Joshua and also in the Book of Judges, was slow and complicated.

When the land was divided (chapters 13—21), part of the tribes had no trouble choosing the territory they wanted. Other tribes were indecisive. To complete the settlement Joshua ordered that three men from each of the unsettled tribes travel over the unclaimed land and write descriptions of it. From the descriptions a map was developed, and the land divided into appropriate sections. Names were drawn to determine which area should be assigned to which tribe. In the final decision two and one-half tribes settled east of the Jordan as had been decided earlier. The remaining nine and one-half tribes settled between the Jordan River and the Mediterranean Sea. (See chart 7.)

The final portion of Joshua (chapters 22—24) describes a renewing of the covenant as the people promised to follow the God of their ancestors, the one who had brought them safely from Egypt into the land that had been promised to Abraham so long ago. They gathered at Shechem and reaffirmed the pledge that had been made at Sinai. Joshua spoke, reviewing the main events of Israelite history and speaking of the "great signs in our sight" (Josh. 24:17) that the Lord had performed. Through mighty acts the Lord had proved himself to be God. Now the time had come for Israel to choose whether they would serve the God who had exhibited such power. Joshua announced his own choice—"As for me and my house, we will serve the Lord" (Josh. 24:15). And in response the people announced their choice—"The Lord our God we will serve, and his voice we will obey" (Josh. 24:24).

"And Israel served the Lord all the days of Joshua, and all the days of the elders who outlived Joshua and had known all the work which the Lord did for Israel" (24:31).

Judges

The Book of Judges is named for thirteen leaders who were called judges, though most filled positions similar to that of guerrilla chieftains. Their primary work was in leading battles, yet some of them acted as town or community counselors.

The Judges Listed in the Book

1. Othniel (3:9)
2. Ehud (3:15)
3. Shamgar (3:31)
4. Deborah (4:4)
5. Gideon (6:19)
6. Abimelech (9:1)
7. Tola (10:1)
8. Jair (10:3)
9. Jephthah (11:1)
10. Ibzan (12:8)
11. Elon (12:11)
12. Abdon (12:13)
13. Samson (13:24)

The opening of Judges shows that the Land of Canaan had not come completely under Israelite control during Joshua's lifetime. Numerous other people lived among and around them—Philistines, Sidonians, Hivites, Hittites, Ammonites, Moabites, Perizzites, Jebusites, Amalakites, Midianites, Amorites (3:3-5). These people followed a religion closely associated with fertility—the reproduction of plants and animals. They set up places of worship on hills, spoken of as "high places." At each high place a tree represented Ashtaroth, the female god, and a stone altar was built to Baal, the male god. To these gods worshipers often sacrificed a child, the fruit of their own fertility, in the hope of promoting the fertility of their fields and flocks (Jer. 19:5). Children were also sacrificed to the idol Molech (Lev. 18:21).

During Joshua's lifetime the Israelites did not become involved in the religion of the Baals and Ashtaroths, but after him "there arose another generation . . . who did not know the Lord or the work which he had done for Israel. And the people of Israel did what was evil in the sight of the Lord . . . and served the Baals and the Ashtaroth" (2:10-11,13). When they stopped serving the Lord, the Lord stopped taking care of them. One or more neighboring tribes attacked one or more Israelite tribes. Israelite crops were destroyed, Israelite villages were set on fire, and Israelites were forced to become slaves of the attackers. When that happened, a judge (leader) arose who led the Israelites to rebel against the attackers and regain freedom. Freedom lasted as long as the judge lived, then the cycle repeated itself.

The judges in the Book of Judges are presented through that recurring pattern: the Israelites turned from God to the religion of the Baals; as a result God abandoned them, and they were conquered by an enemy; a judge led a successful revolt against the enemy; the people served God as long as the judge lived then "they turned back and behaved worse than their fathers" (Judg. 2:19).

The judges were gifted individuals who became heroes among their own people. They lived during the chaotic period of Israelite adjustment from nomads to farmers and villagers. There was no central government: "There was no king in Israel; every man did what was right in his own eyes" (Judg. 21:25). The age was one of unrest and violence, not one of political or spiritual advance. Morals were low, and generations failed to pass what they had learned to succeeding generations. The writer of Judges, however, used the recurring pattern of Israelite behavior to demonstrate the same lesson over and over: when the people followed God, they were blessed; when they turned away, they suffered.

Ruth

Ruth contains the beautiful story of a young Moabite woman who lived at the same time as the Judges. She is important in the biblical record because she married into the family of Judah, and her great-grandson became the famous King David.

In addition to providing a link in the historical story, Ruth is important because the book illustrates a theological point. It shows that King David came from a racial mixture. At various times the Book of Ruth has been used to point out that the God of the Bible is concerned, not with a pure race, but with pure attitudes and motives; with what a person is like, not with whom one's father or mother were, or where they came from.

Daily Bible Reading Schedule

Week 6
Josh. 1:1-18
Josh. 2
Josh. 3
Josh. 4
Josh. 6:1-25
Josh. 18:1-10
Josh. 23:1-3; 24:14-28

Week 7
Judg. 2:7-20
Judg. 6:1-24
Judg. 6:25-40; 7:1-8,19-20; 21:25
Ruth 1
Ruth 2
Ruth 3
Ruth 4

Suggested Topics for Further Research

Akhnaton: a pharaoh of ancient Egypt who changed Egypt's religion
Baal, Ashtaroth: gods of the ancient Canaanites
Dead Sea: sea into which the Jordan empties
Habiru: nomadic people mentioned in ancient literature
Hexateuch: the first five books of the Bible plus Joshua
Hieroglyphics: writing of the ancient Egyptians
Hittites: ancient people who established a nation in what is presently Turkey
Jericho: one of the world's oldest cities
Jordan River: river flowing through the heart of Canaan
Mount Gerizim and Mount Ebal: mountains in central Canaan
Rameses: a pharaoh of ancient Egypt
Sea of Galilee: small lake through which flows the Jordan River
Tel-el-Amarna letters: letters from people in Canaan to a pharaoh
Troy: ancient city engaged in wars with the Greeks about the same time that the Israelites were settling in Canaan. (The Trojan horse story came out of wars taking place at approximately the same time as the period of the Judges in the Bible.)

Reinforce Your Memory

Joshua records the account of the Israelites as they _____ in Canaan. The book has three sections. The first tells about the _____ of the land, the second shows how the land was _____, and the third contains _____ that Joshua made to the people.

Judges is named for _____ leaders who led one or more of the Israelite tribes at various times. Review in your mind the chaotic times of the judges, why, and the lesson to be learned from the recurring pattern of behavior demonstrated in the book.

The Book of Ruth is about a young woman from _____ who lived at the time of the judges. She is important largely because she was the great-grandmother of _____.

Draw a timeline and mark the approximate time of Joshua.

Draw a map similar to chart 7. Designate the area where two and one-half tribes settled and the area where the other nine and one-half tribes settled.

Chart 8.
1 Samuel, 2 Samuel, 1 Kings 1—11

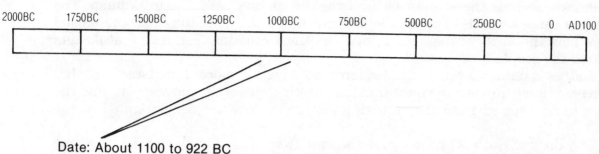

2000BC   1750BC   1500BC   1250BC   1000BC   750BC   500BC   250BC   0   AD100

Date: About 1100 to 922 BC

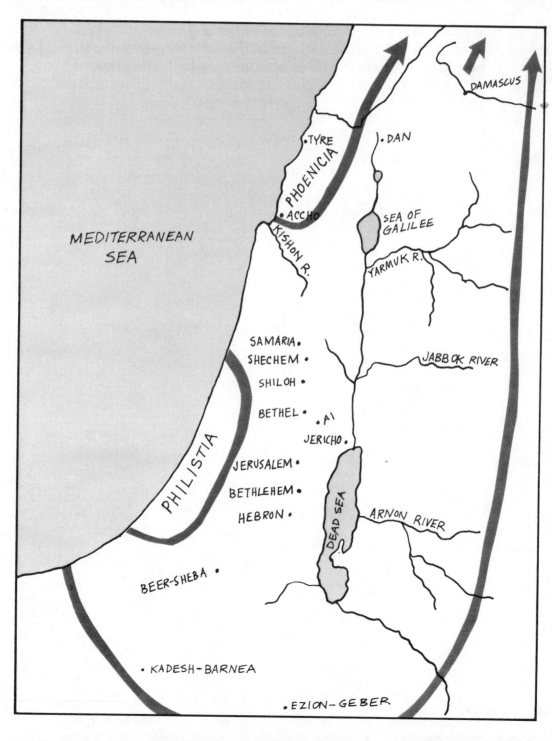

MEDITERRANEAN
SEA

PHOENICIA

•TYRE

•DAN

•ACCHO

KISHON R.

SEA OF
GALILEE

YARMUK R.

SAMARIA•
SHECHEM •
SHILOH •
BETHEL •
•AI
JERICHO •

JABBOK RIVER

JERUSALEM •
BETHLEHEM •
HEBRON •

DEAD SEA

ARNON RIVER

PHILISTIA

BEER-SHEBA •

•KADESH-BARNEA

•EZION-GEBER

DAMASCUS

What the Books of Samuel and Kings Are About

In the Hebrew Scriptures 1 and 2 Samuel were originally one book filling one scroll. Around 200 BC a Greek translation was made. Unlike ancient Hebrew, Greek had vowels, therefore more writing space was required. Because of that, Samuel was divided into two scrolls. The Books of Kings were also one book, and they too became two scrolls in the Greek translation.

Although Samuel and Kings became four books in the Greek translation, they were all grouped together under one title, "The Books of the Kingdoms." Many years later, around AD 400, a Latin translation was made. It also grouped the four books together but called them "The Books of the Kings." Both titles were well chosen because they each give clues as to what the books are about.

The opening of 1 Samuel shows that the Israelites had reached a turning point in their existence. They had come a long way from their early beginning told about in Genesis. During the time told about in Exodus they had become a united people who had entered into a covenant with God. Numbers records the years they spent as nomads. Joshua tells of their going into their Promised Land and establishing permanent homes. Judges tells of the chaotic first centuries in that land as they shifted from nomads to agriculturalists. The Books of Samuel and Kings tell of the next series of steps in their history, a series of steps concerned with kings and kingdoms. The time covered in the books is slightly more than five hundred years, from about 1050 BC to about 550 BC.

1 Samuel

Both 1 and 2 Samuel are named for a man who filled a position halfway between that of a judge and that of a king. In addition he was looked upon as a priest. Samuel was probably better known by members of all twelve Israelite tribes than any of the thirteen judges in the Book of Judges. He was the strongest and most respected leader the Israelites had had since Moses and Joshua. He was the last of his kind of leader, the ones who led but who were not kings. He served during the transition time between the judges and the kings; he touched both the old and the new order.

The new order was, of course, the beginning of the kings. The Israelites decided to elect a king over Samuel's strong objections. He told them the disadvantages— the high cost of supporting a king who would have to have servants and chariots, equipment for war and for entertaining, officers for his government and taxes from everybody. Samuel was usually listened to, and his advice taken, but he was ineffective in preventing the election of a king.

The Israelites' desire for a king was actually a desire for an effective army. By joining together they hoped to develop enough military power to end the constant harassment they had endured from neighboring tribes throughout the years of the judges. (In a sense Israelite history was similar to American history as it developed into a united nation. Thirteen American colonies joined together to form the United States just as thirteen Israelite tribes joined to form a country that is usually spoken of as the United Kingdom. The American colonies united to help each other; the Israelites felt the same need.) The beginning of the years of Israelite kings came at approximately the same time as the beginning of the Iron Age. The people who troubled the Israelites most were the Philistines who had developed a small nation on the coast of the Mediterranean Sea right next to Israel. The Philistines knew how to make iron, a skill that made them dominant in the area. The Israelites not only had to go to Philistia to buy plows, axes, sickles, and mattocks, but they had to go there to have them sharpened. (See 1 Sam. 13:19-22.) The Philistines had swords, and their chariots had iron wheels; the Israelites resented their own weak status in comparison. They thought that if they chose a king he might be able to build a strong enough army from the united tribes to make their position less vulnerable.

Saul, the king the Israelites chose, did what was expected of him. He organized an army and fought. "He fought aginst all his enemies on every side, . . . wherever he turned he put them to the worse. And he did valiantly, . . . and delivered Israel out of the hands of those who plundered them" (1 Sam. 14:47-48). The Book of 1 Samuel could easily be called the Book of the First King of Israel, for more than anything else it tells about the reign of Saul as the first king.

> The United Kingdom
> First King: Saul

In addition to Samuel and Saul, 1 Samuel introduces one other important personality—David. David became commander in chief of Saul's army, the best friend of Saul's son Jonathan, and so popular with the Israelite people that Saul developed a fanatical jealousy of him.

Saul became convinced that David was attempting to usurp the throne and therefore spent more time trying to annihilate David than in fighting the enemies of Israel. In addition to his jealousy, Saul experienced mental and spiritual instability, feeling that God had abandoned him. He had courage and strength to lead his army against massive odds, yet suffered tragically from inner turmoils. Nevertheless, Saul accomplished much. He had no organized system of draft, but when he "saw any strong man, or any valiant man, he attached him to himself" (1 Sam. 14:52). He made substantial progress toward freeing Israel of harassment. He lacked the skill and popularity of David, but he had the loyalty of his troops and the ability to accomplish what his people asked him to do when they named him king.

2 Samuel

Second Samuel could easily be called the Book of the Second King because it covers the reign of David as the second king of the United Kingdom. The book is one of the easiest portions of the entire Old Testament to read and comprehend.

> The United Kingdom
> First King: Saul
> Second King: David

David was disliked by few and loved by many. A genius in political diplomacy as well as in military skills, he won the loyalty of his people long before he became king. After Saul's jealousy made it necessary for him to stop leading battles for Saul, he continued to fight against enemies of his country; and whenever he captured anything of value he sent gifts to the officials of Israelite cities. In addition, with the small army that attached itself to him, he protected farms and grazing lands of Israelites who lived along the borders of the country. Too, he won the admiration of people because he always supported Saul regardless of how Saul treated him.

Second Samuel covers the history of David from just after Saul's death till just before David himself died about forty years later. Besides David, the most prominent person in the book is Joab, David's nephew who was commander in chief of David's army and essentially David's right hand man. Several times Joab had to jar David to his senses when the king was moved more by emotion than by reason. A number of other people are important in the book: Ishbosheth, Saul's son; Abner, Isbosheth's army commander; Mephibosheth, Jonathan's son; Zadok and Abiathar, priests; several of David's children, especially Tamar, a daughter, and sons, Amnon and Absalom; and Bathsheba who became David's wife later in his life after he made the grievous mistake of becoming involved with her and having her husband killed.

David is sometimes called the architect of the Israelite state. He had a full organized cabinet (see 2 Sam. 8:15-18) and expanded the borders of the country until it became a leading nation among the small countries surrounding it. David's military brilliance is commonly accepted as his means of success, yet his attainments can be attributed as much to diplomacy as to martial skill.

One effective step that David took toward cementing unity among the tribes of his own country was in the establishment of Jerusalem as the capital. Jerusalem, although in the heart of the Israelites' land, had never been conquered by the Israelites. It belonged to the Jebusites, and for years the city had stood as an invincible fort. Soon after David became king he conquered it, demonstrating to the people of Israel that the new king was able to accomplish feats others had considered impossible.

David's choice of Jerusalem as the nation's capital was wise for several reasons. The city was well located and easy to defend, but more importantly it was not in a territory that belonged to any of the Israelite tribes. If he had chosen as capital a city belonging to one of the tribes, there might have been jealousy. By choosing Jerusalem he showed no favoritism. (Like Washington DC, Jerusalem was on neutral ground.)

David not only made Jerusalem the political capital but also made it the religious center of the country. He bought property and collected materials for building a temple. The property he purchased was the location where it is believed that Abraham took Isaac to be sacrificed centuries before. (See Gen. 22:1-14.) Today the Muslim temple, the Dome of the Rock, stands on the site. A railing inside the temple encircles the rock believed to have been the place where Abraham was to sacrifice Isaac before God intervened. Although he had to leave the actual construction of the Temple to Solomon, David did cause Jerusalem to become the religious center of the country.

David's abilities, and achievements, did not cause his reign to run smoothly. His spoiled sons repeatedly disrupted affairs. And he had major problems with some of his cabinet members. Nevertheless, his winsomeness, his faith in God, and his accomplishments gave David an unparalleled place in Israelite history.

1 Kings 1-11

First Kings 1 through 11 continues the account of the United Kingdom by telling about Solomon's reign as the third king of the United Kingdom.

> The United Kingdom
>
> First King: Saul
> Second King: David
> Third King: Solomon

Solomon is noted for both his wisdom and his building projects. Under him the little country reached its zenith.

Solomon's personal fame stretched to distant lands. He wrote many psalms and proverbs. And he increased the size of his nation till it stretched from the Euphrates River to the borders of Egypt.

Several ruins of his building projects exist today, the best known being remains of copper mines at Ezion-geber, a city at the southern coast. The most famous of his projects was the construction of the Temple, a small but exquisite structure located next to the palace and other governmental buildings.

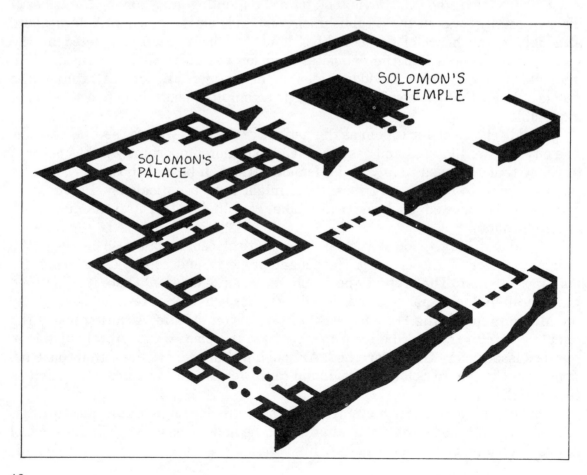

For his many projects Solomon needed money, and to get money he utilized two main sources. One helped the country, the other did irreparable damage.

The good source came through taking advantage of his country's location. Because it was between countries that needed supplies Solomon acted as middleman, importing goods from the south, exporting them to the north at a profit and vice versa. (See 1 Kings 10:28-29.)

The unwise source came through excessive taxes and forced labor. He divided his own country into twelve parts, not along the tribal divisions, but into new groupings for the purpose of taxation. Each part had to support the king's household one month out of each twelve. (For materials each area had to supply see 1 Kings 4:20-22,28.) In addition, laborers were forced to spend one month out of every three working on Solomon's projects. (See 1 Kings 5:13-17; 9:22.) The demands became so extensive that a feeling of mutiny began rising among the Israelites. Solomon "excelled all the kings of the earth in riches and wisdom" (1 Kings 10:23), but in making "silver as common in Jerusalem as stone" (1 Kings 10:27) he damaged his people.

Late in his life Solomon turned from the principles that had made him great. He had married many wives. Some of the marriages were diplomatic arrangements. To please his wives he built temples to their gods and began burning incense in honor of the gods. "And the Lord was angry with Solomon, because his heart had turned away from the Lord" (1 Kings 11:9).

During Solomon's final years, his reign was in jeopardy. Several groups rose up against him and Ahijah predicted that the kingdom would be torn away from Solomon's son, leaving only a small portion and given to Jeroboam, a man who was an overseer of some of Solomon's building projects. Ahijah was wearing a new garment which he took and tore into twelve pieces. He handed ten pieces to Jeroboam saying, "Thus says the Lord, the God of Israel, 'Behold I am about to tear the kingdom from the hand of Solomon, and will give you ten tribes . . . because he has forsaken me, . . . and has not walked in my ways. . . . Nevertheless I will not take the whole kingdom out of his hand; but I will make him ruler all the days of his life, for the sake of David my servant whom I chose, who kept my commandments and my statutes; but I will take the kingdom out of his son's hand, and will give it to you, ten tribes" (1 Kings 11:31-36). Solomon tried to kill Jeroboam, but Jeroboam fled to Egypt where he stayed until Solomon died (v. 40).

Reinforce Your Memory

The reign of _____ as the first king of the United Kingdom is recorded in _____.

The reign of _____ as the second king of the United Kingdom is recorded in _____.

The reign of _____ as the third king of the United Kingdom is recorded in _____.

Draw a timeline showing the approximate time covered during the reigns of the three kings.

In the space below draw a map showing the location and size of the United Kingdom under King David. Mark on it the capital city he established.

Chart 9.
1 Kings 12—2 Kings 16

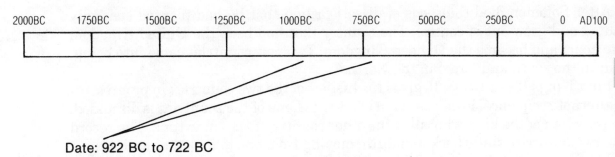

2000BC 1750BC 1500BC 1250BC 1000BC 750BC 500BC 250BC 0 AD100

Date: 922 BC to 722 BC

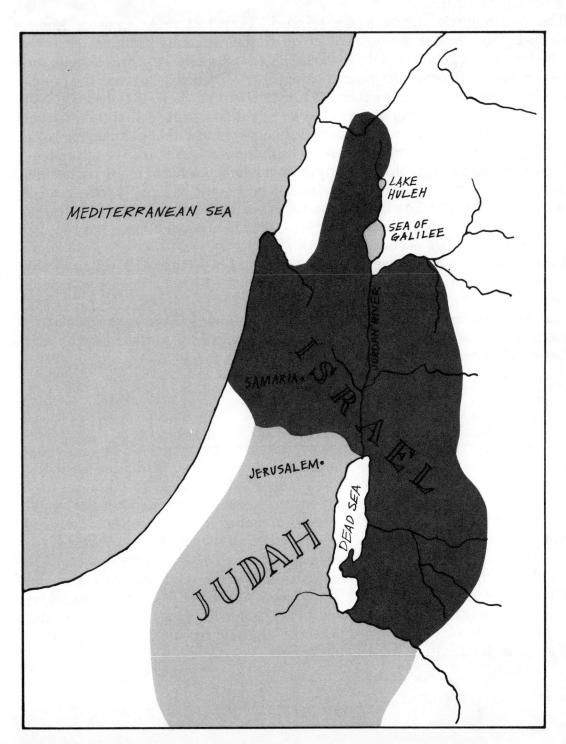

MEDITERRANEAN SEA

LAKE HULEH

SEA OF GALILEE

JORDAN RIVER

SAMARIA·

ISRAEL

JERUSALEM·

DEAD SEA

JUDAH

1 Kings 12—2 Kings 16

After Solomon died the seeds of dissatisfaction that he had planted suddenly sprouted and grew out of control. The country that had been the United Kingdom broke apart and became the Divided Kingdom. Two new countries came into being, Judah in the south and Israel in the North.

First Kings 12—2 Kings 16 gives the history of the two countries in progressive and alternate sequence. First the reign of a king of one of the countries is discussed, then the reign of the king who ruled the other country at the same time. The record of the two countries shifts back and forth, moving from one to the other each time a new king rose to the throne.

The two countries never again rejoined. They had their separate kings, established their separate capitals, and produced their separate histories.

The kingdom split apart at what should have been a celebration. Solomon's son Rehoboam went to Shechem for his coronation service. When he arrived, the people asked him to be less severe on them than Solomon had been. If Rehoboam had realized just how tense a situation existed he might have agreed, and there would have been shouts of "Long live the king." But he announced that he intended to be more strict than Solomon, and the ten tribes withdrew from the union shouting they would have nothing to do with the family of David. Rehoboam had to flee for his life.

Jeroboam, the man the prophet Ahijah had said would be king, became head of the ten tribes (12:21-25). The two remaining tribes, Judah and Benjamin, allowed Rehoboam to continue as their king, not because of Rehoboam himself but because they wanted a decendant of David on the throne.

Rehoboam's country became known as the Southern Kingdom as well as by the name Judah. Jerusalem continued to serve as both the political and religious capital.

The new country formed by the ten tribes became known as the Northern Kingdom as well as Israel. Shechem became the temporary political capital, and Jeroboam set up two new religious centers.

The Divided Kingdom	
Israel (the Northern Kingdom)	10 tribes
Judah (the Southern Kingdom)	2 tribes

Jeroboam established the new religious centers because he did not want the people of his new country going to Jerusalem to worship. He was afraid that if they went to Jerusalem they might want to reunite the country with Rehoboam as king. To prevent that he announced that new worship centers had been put in convenient locations, one at Dan in the north and the other at Bethel on the main road to Jerusalem. At each of the shrines he set up a golden calf. He probably intended that the people worship God as the unseen deity riding above the animals. But the Israelites looked upon the calves as gods. For that reason Jeroboam is often spoken of in the Bible as the king who "made Israel to sin" (1 Kings 15:26,34). At the religious centers anyone who wished to be a priest could become one. No hereditary priesthood like the Levitical was established.

Because of Jeroboam's new religious centers, the Levites all left the Northern Kingdom and went south to Judah where they continued to serve as religious leaders just as they had ever since the establishment of the Levitical priesthood (2 Chron. 11:13-17).

The Divided Kingdom existed for approximately two hundred years. During that time Judah had thirteen different kings. (See king list, chart 10.) All of them came from the family of David except Athaliah, a woman who ruled for a brief time. Few of the kings were commendable leaders; most were bad. All ruled from Jerusalem.

Israel, at the same time, had nineteen different kings. They came from seven different families. New dynasties usually came into power through assassinating the current king and his family. Those responsible for the assassination usually chose who would be king. Not one of the kings is described as good. Several of them established new capitals, but Omri, the sixth king and one of the strongest, bought land and began building the capital that became permanent for the rest of the period that the country existed. Omri's son Ahab continued the construction of the city, called Samaria. The new capital was strategically located and well protected. It became wealthy and influential. It was sometimes called the city of ivory because so much ivory was used as inlay in furniture and paneled walls. (Today fragments of ivory litter the site of the ancient city.)

Ahab ruled during one of the most prosperous periods in Israel's history. It was also one of the most religiously corrupt. (Ahab was married to the wicked Queen Jezebel whose name has become proverbial in connection with evil.)

The prophets Elijah and Elisha were prominent during Ahab's reign. They were among a series of prophets who arose as God's speakers against the religious corruption in both Israel and Judah.

The period of the Divided Kingdom was a time of alternate peace and war. Sometimes Judah and Israel fought with each other. Sometimes they fought wars against other small countries around them. Sometimes they joined with each other to fight a common enemy. During those years the nation of Assyria began developing in the area between the Tigris and Euphrates rivers. It attacked small countries near it, taking over one after another, and soon began to loom over Israel and Judah like a dark cloud certain to bring a storm.

Chart 10.
Kings of the Divided Kingdom

Judah		Israel	
Ruler	Date ruled	Ruler	Date ruled
Rehoboam	922-915 BC*	Jeroboam I	922-901 BC
Abijah	915-913		
Asa	913-873	Nadab	901-900
		Baasha	900-877
		Elah	877-876
		Zimri	876
Jehoshaphat	873-849	Omri	876-869
		Ahab	869-850
Jehoram	849-842	Ahaziah	850-849
Ahaziah	842	Joram	849-842
Athaliah	842-837	Jehu	842-815
Jehoash	837-800	Jehoahaz	815-801
Amaziah	800-783	Joash	801-786
Uzziah	783-742	Jeroboam II	786-746
Jotham	742-735	Zechariah	746-745
		Shallum	745
		Menahem	745-738
		Pekahiah	738-737
Ahaz	735-715	Pekah	737-732
Hezekiah	715-687	Hoshea	732-724
		Fall of Samaria: 722	

With the fall of Samaria the country of Israel ceased to exist. Judah survived another hundred years.

Last kings of Judah

Ruler	Date ruled
Manasseh	687-642
Amon	642-640
Josiah	640-609
Shallum	609
Jehoiakim	609-597
Jehoiachin	598
Zedekiah	598-587

*All dates are approximate

Reinforce Your Memory

After Solomon's death, the United Kingdom split into two parts, a Northern Kingdom made up of _____ tribes and a Southern Kingdom made up of _____ tribes.

The Northern Kingdom was named _____, and its permanent capital was _____.

The Southern Kingdom was named _____, and its capital was _____. The history of the two kingdoms is given in _____.

Two important prophets told about in the same section are _____ and _____.

What format does the Bible use in telling about the two countries?

Draw a timeline and mark the beginning date of the Divided Kingdom.

In the space below draw a map showing the two countries that made up the Divided Kingdom. Label them and mark their capital cities.

Chart 11.
2 Kings 17—20

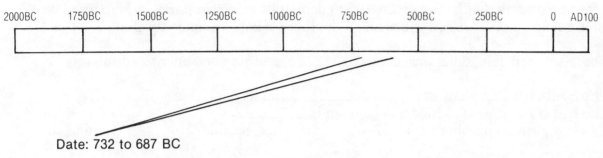

| 2000BC | 1750BC | 1500BC | 1250BC | 1000BC | 750BC | 500BC | 250BC | 0 | AD100 |

Date: 732 to 687 BC

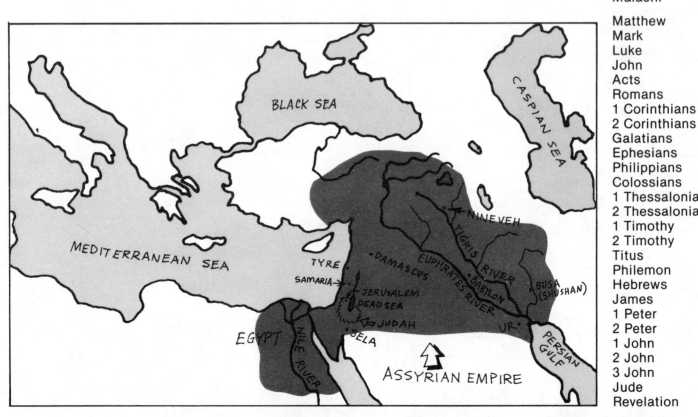

Second Kings 17—20 covers the reigns of only two kings, Hoshea of Israel and Hezekiah of Judah. (See king list, chart 10.) Their reigns are extremely important because while they ruled both Israel and Judah were attacked by the nation of Assyria.

Assyria was the first of five powerful empires that affected the lives of biblical people between the time of the Divided Kingdom and the time of Christ. The five nations each brought such sweeping changes among biblical people that some scholars refer to them as the "March of the Empires."

> **The March of the Empires**
> **First: Assyria**

The Assyrian nation was probably begun by farmers who lived in what is now Russia but pushed south looking for better agricultural lands. By the time they took what they wanted, war had become a way of life for them.

The Assyrians are known as some of the most ruthless people who ever lived. A typical inscription written by one of their kings says, "I took prisoners. Of some I cut off the feet and hands, of others I cut off the noses, ears, and lips; of the young men's ears I made a heap; of the old men's heads I built a tower." Many scenes from battles the Assyrians fought can be seen among the ruins of their once magnificent cities. One shows Assyrian soldiers gaining access to a city by swimming underwater, using the inflated skins of sheep as air tanks.

The matchless hordes of Assyrian soldiers, wearing pointed hats and kiltlike skirts, comprised the world's first army that was fully equipped with iron weapons. Yet the nation's success was due only in part to weapons and numbers of soldiers. Equally important were leaders with ideas.

One idea the Assyrians used was effective because it broke down the nationalistic feelings of peoples they conquered. Prisoners taken from one area were never allowed to stay together en mass but were separated into small groups. Each group was sent to a different part of the empire. Because they did not know the language or customs of the new area there was little chance any group would rebel against Assyria. By the time individuals learned to communicate well they had become a part of their new location. Most groups became so intermingled with others that they lost their national identity.

During the reign of Hoshea, the Assyrian army attacked the country of Israel. The city of Samaria managed to hold out for three years but finally fell. With the fall of Samaria the country of Israel came to an end. The date was 722 BC, almost exactly 200 years after the country began.

The people of Israel were sent to several different parts of the Assyrian Empire (see 2 Kings 17:6). In those scattered places they became so mixed with people of other nationalities that they became known as "the ten lost tribes." They never returned to their own country as a unified people again. Their distinction as a separate people was lost.

Not only were the people of Israel sent to faraway places, but people were brought into Israel from distant lands (see 2 Kings 17:24). A new mixed nationality arose. The new people gradually acquired the named *Samaritan* because they lived in the vicinity of the destroyed city of Samaria. (Later the country became known as Samaria instead of Israel.)

After conquering Israel, the Assyrians marched south intending to take Judah. They burned several cities, then surrounded Jerusalem.

Hezekiah, king of Judah, was one of the best kings Judah ever had. He prepared his country for war; an evidence of his preparation that can still be seen today is an underground tunnel designed to bring water from outside the walls into the city in case of a seige. The tunnel was an engineering marvel for that day; workers started at opposite ends and cut through solid rock, successfully meeting in the middle.

When the Assyrians surrounded Jerusalem, Hezekiah sent a message to the prophet Isaiah telling him of the threat to the city. Isaiah sent back word saying God would cause the king to return to his own land, and Jerusalem would be saved.

A short time later Hezekiah received a letter from Sennacherib, king of Assyria. In the letter Sennacherib bragged about the many countries his people had conquered. He reminded Hezekiah that all the countries he had defeated had gods but the gods, as well as the cities, had been burned. He suggested that Hezekiah not foolishly rely on his God, but to use good sense and surrender.

Hezekiah went into the Temple, spread the letter before the Lord, and began to pray:

> Incline thy ear, O Lord, and hear; open thy eyes, O Lord, and see; and hear the words of Sennacherib, which he has sent to mock the living God. Of a truth, O Lord, the kings of Assyria have laid waste the nations and their lands, and have cast their gods into fire; for they were no gods, but the work of men's hands, wood and stone; therefore they were destroyed. So now, O Lord our God, save us, I beseech thee, from his hand, that all the kingdoms of the earth may know that thou, O Lord, art God alone (2 Kings 19:16-19).

That night a sudden illness swept through the Assyrian camp. So many soldiers died that the survivors grew too frightened to stay in the area. They crept back to their homeland, and Judah was left undefeated, a tiny island in a sea of Assyrian power.

Among the Assyrian records still existing is a carving giving Sennacherib's own account of the war against Jerusalem. He bragged that he shut Hezekiah "up like a caged bird within Jerusalem, his royal city"; yet he admitted that Hezekiah "did not bow in submission to my yoke." (Documents From Old Testament Times, edited by D. Winton Thomas, p. 67, First Harper Torchbook edition, 1961, Harper and Row, Publishers, New York.)

Reinforce Your Memory

During the reign of _____, the nineteenth king of Israel, the _____ _____ conquered the city of _____, and the country of Israel came to an end.

The people of Israel were scattered in so many places that they became known as _____ _____ _____ _____.

_____ attacked Judah also, intending to destroy it but did not succeed. The King of Judah at that time was _____, one of the best kings the country ever had. The king was greatly influenced by _____, perhaps the best known of all biblical prophets.

Draw a timeline and mark on it the date of the fall of Israel.

Draw a map outlining the Assyrian Empire and showing the little country of Judah in the midst of the great Assyrian nation.

Chart 12.
2 Kings 21—25

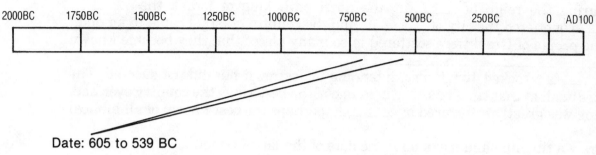

2000BC	1750BC	1500BC	1250BC	1000BC	750BC	500BC	250BC	0 AD100

Date: 605 to 539 BC

BLACK SEA

CASPIAN SEA

MEDITERRANEAN SEA

TIGRIS RIVER

BABYLON

EUPHRATES RIVER

DEAD SEA

EGYPT

NILE R.

RED SEA

BABYLONIAN EMPIRE

PERSIAN GULF

The country of Judah survived about a hundred years longer than the country of Israel. Then it, too, fell. Second Kings 21—25 tells about the final years of Judah and of its fall.

During the hundred years between the fall of Israel and the fall of Judah, seven kings ruled Judah. The two most important of those seven were Manasseh and Josiah. Manasseh was important because he was bad, Josiah because he was good.

Last Seven Kings of Judah

Manasseh (reigned 55 years)
Amon (reigned 2 years)
Josiah (reigned 31 years)
Jehoahaz (reigned 3 months)
Jehoiakim (reigned 11 years)
Jehoiachin (reigned 3 months)
Zedekiah (reigned 11 years)

Mannasseh ruled longer than any of the other kings of Judah, and he also caused more religious corruption than any of the other kings. His evil leadership is listed as the major cause of the downfall of his country.

Manasseh's grandson Josiah, in contrast, was one of the few kings of Judah who is described as truly good. He ordered that the Temple be cleaned and remodeled. During the restoration an important discovery was made. The high priest found "the book of the law" and sent it to Josiah (2 Kings 22:8). (Many scholars believe the book was Deuteronomy.) When Josiah heard the words in the book he began a massive religious reform. He destroyed idolatrous places of worship throughout the land, had the book that had been found taught to the people, and observed the Passover festival (2 Kings 23:1-23).

There were many idolatrous places that had to be destroyed: people burned incense to Baal, to the sun, moon, and the constellations; in the valley of Hinnom they burned their children as offerings to Molech; the altar at Bethel where Jeroboam had set up a golden calf was still being used. Josiah succeeded in destroying them, but he did not succeed in changing the people. He was killed in battle, and the kings who followed him "did what was evil in the sight of the Lord" (2 Kings 23:32). The last years of the kingdom were ones of internal decay. The country was defeated by the Babylonian Empire.

The Babylonian Empire was the second of the series of five powerful empires that affected biblical people between the time of the Divided Kingdom and the time of Christ. It began in the Mesopotamian region near where Abraham had originally lived. It gradually took over all that had belonged to Assyria. The nation was named

---

The March of the Empires

First: Assyria
Second: Babylonia

---

for its capital city, the fabulous Babylon, famous for its hanging gardens, one of the seven wonders of the ancient world. Ruins of the city's massive walls, once covered with blue glazed tile, still stand.

Babylonia reached its highest attainment under Nebuchadnezzar who ruled from around 605 to 562 BC. It was he who had the hanging gardens built, and it was under him that the city of Jerusalem was defeated.

Nebuchadnezzar's army attacked Jerusalem several different times. The first attack was designed only to bring the city under Babylonian control and make the people pay taxes to Babylon. The second attack came when the king of Judah refused to pay the taxes. Following that attack the cream of Jerusalem's society, many of the skilled workers and trained people, were captured and taken to Babylon, including the king and his mother (2 Kings 24:11-16). Only the weakest and poorest people were left in Jerusalem, yet even that group rebelled against Babylon. Nebuchadnezzar then sent a final attack on the city, and Jerusalem was reduced to ruins in 587 BC.

Unlike the Assyrians, the Babylonians did not try to destroy the national identity of peoples they conquered. Citizens of a country were not separated from each other but lived in an area together. They were given jobs according to their skills and were allowed to practice their own religion. Because of that leniency, the people of Judah did not become "lost" tribes but remained a distinct people. They did, however, acquire a nickname. They became known as Jews.

Second Kings ends with the Jews in Babylon. They were only a fraction of what they might have been had there been fewer upheavals in their history. Yet that fraction—remnant as it is often called—felt and showed a unity unparalleled among other people. They were a people of one God, a people of one history, and they longed to be a people of one land, the land promised to Abraham so long ago.

(Although they are not mentioned in 2 Kings, the prophets Jeremiah and Ezekiel were two of the most important people at the time of the Babylonian Empire. In world history, the time of Jeremiah and Ezekiel was close to the time of Confucius and Buddha. Socrates was born about a hundred years later.)

The time the Jews spent in Babylon, approximately seventy years from the first attack by Nebuchadnezzar until they were freed, is usually referred to as the Babylonian captivity or the Exile. Those years were not barren for the Jews. During that time they learned that God could be anywhere, not just in the Promised Land. They learned that before they became a nation they were a covenant people, and the covenant lived on even when the nation did not. The covenant, however, was not only with the people as a unit, but with individuals who made up the unit. Each person needed to be a priest, and each needed to look beyond his or her own community to the world. Some Jews began to recognize that their nation had been chosen, not because God loved them more than all others, but because God loved all people, and they were to share that news. After the years in Babylon, the Jews, who before then had fluctuated in their faith, turning as often to idols as to God, permanently gave up idolatry. Idols have not since been a part of their lives. Babylon was far from the homeland they loved, but it did not prove to be a wasteland; there Jewish faith was fertilized.

Daily Bible Reading Schedule

Week 8
1 Sam. 7:15 to 8:22
1 Sam. 10:17-27
1 Sam. 13:1,19-22; 14:4-23
1 Sam. 17:32-49
1 Sam. 18:6-16; 19:8-10
1 Sam. 27:1-4; 29:1-7,11
1 Sam. 31:1-13

Week 9
2 Sam. 1:2-12
2 Sam. 2:1-11; 4:5 to 5:10
2 Sam. 7:1-17; 8:15-18
2 Sam. 15:1-14
2 Sam. 18:1-18
2 Sam. 19:1-15
1 Kings 1:1-31

Week 10
1 Kings 1:32-40
1 Kings 2:12; 3:1-15
1 Kings 4:21-34
1 Kings 5:1-18
1 Kings 6:1-13
1 Kings 7:1-12
1 Kings 11:4-13,26-41

Week 11
1 Kings 12:1-17
1 Kings 12:18-33
1 Kings 13:1-10; 14:19-24
1 Kings 15:9-34
1 Kings 16:5-33
1 Kings 18
1 Kings 22:40-53

Week 12
2 Kings 3:1-24
2 Kings 8:16-27
2 Kings 9:1-13
2 Kings 12:1-15,19
2 Kings 13:1-13
2 Kings 14:1-22
2 Kings 15:1-15

Week 13
2 Kings 17:1-18
2 Kings 17:24-41
2 Kings 18:1-2,16-17
2 Kings 18:28 to 19:1,14-20,35-36
2 Kings 21:1-18
2 Kings 22 to 23:5
2 Kings 24:1-15; 25:8-11

Suggested Topics for Further Research

Gibeah: Saul's capital, first political center of United Kingdom
Philistia: country beside United Kingdom
Jerusalem: capital David established
Solomon's Temple: Temple built by Solomon in Jerusalem
Dome of the Rock: Muslim Temple on site of Solomon's former Temple
Ezion-geber: seaport at time of Solomon
Megiddo: city in central part of United Kingdom
Samaria: capital of Israel built by Omri and Ahab
Moabite Stone: commemorative stone of a Moabite king
Chemosh, Molech, Baal: gods worshiped by neighbors of the Israelites
Assyrian Empire: nation that conquered Israel
Babylonian Empire: nation that conquered Judah

Reinforce Your Memory

The _____ Empire was the second of the great nations to affect the people of the Bible between the time of the Divided Kingdom and the time of Christ.

The empire was named for its capital city, _____, famous for its _____ _____. The nation reached its highest attainment under King _____.

After the Babylonian War the people of Judah became known as _____.

Although only a _____ of their former size, the Jews did not become "lost tribes" like the people of Israel but retained their identity as a distinct people.

Draw a timeline and mark on it the approximate date of the fall of Jerusalem.

In the space below draw a map showing the outline of the Babylonian Empire. Also locate Jerusalem and Babylon.

Chart 13.
1 and 2 Chronicles, Ezra, Nehemiah, Esther

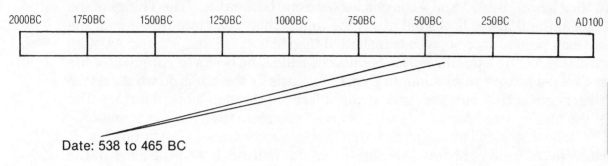

| 2000BC | 1750BC | 1500BC | 1250BC | 1000BC | 750BC | 500BC | 250BC | 0 | AD100 |

Date: 538 to 465 BC

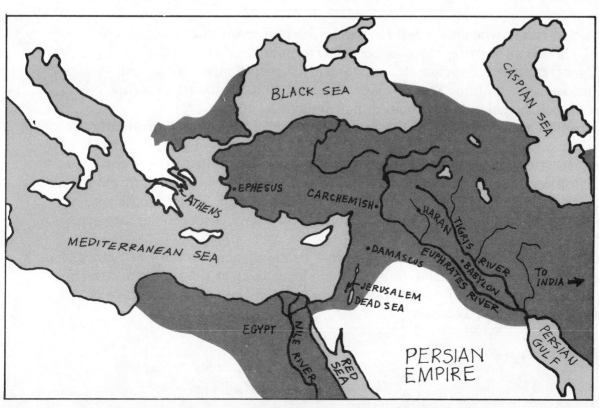

Genesis
Exodus
Leviticus
Numbers
Deuteronomy
Joshua
Judges
Ruth
1 Samuel
2 Samuel
1 Kings
2 Kings
1 Chronicles
2 Chronicles
Ezra
Nehemiah
Esther
Job
Psalms
Proverbs
Ecclesiastes
Song of Solomon
Isaiah
Jeremiah
Lamentations
Ezekiel
Daniel
Hosea
Joel
Amos
Obadiah
Jonah
Micah
Nahum
Habakkuk
Zephaniah
Haggai
Zechariah
Malachi

Matthew
Mark
Luke
John
Acts
Romans
1 Corinthians
2 Corinthians
Galatians
Ephesians
Philippians
Colossians
1 Thessalonians
2 Thessalonians
1 Timothy
2 Timothy
Titus
Philemon
Hebrews
James
1 Peter
2 Peter
1 John
2 John
3 John
Jude
Revelation

1 and 2 Chronicles

In the Hebrew Bible 1 and 2 Chronicles were one book called "The Things of the Days," meaning that the books tell about the things that took place throughout the days of God's people. Jerome, who translated the Bible into Latin around AD 400, is responsible for the title Chronicles because he called the books "a chronicle of the whole of sacred history from Adam to Cyrus." Essentially the books do what Jerome said: they begin with Adam and move straight forward through biblical history. The part of the history from Adam to Saul, however, is no more than a list of names.

The list of names, which covers the first nine chapters of 1 Chronicles, is important to the kind of history the Chronicler was writing. It sets the Jews in the context of progressive world history, yet singles them out from among other people.

Following the list of names, 1 and 2 Chronicles repeat the same history that is given in Samuel and Kings although there are several important differences. The reason for the differences, and also for the repetition, can be understood only through considering when and why the books were written.

Before the writer of Chronicles, who is not known but is usually called "the Chronicler," began writing, one important event took place that is not told about in Kings. It is that Cyrus, king of Persia, conquered Babylon and freed the Jews. Second Kings ends with the Jews in Babylon where they had been taken as prisoners of war; 2 Chronicles adds that Cyrus released them and let them go home.

The Persian Empire, with Cyrus at its head, was the third of the series of five powerful empires that affected the Jews. Cyrus is known as one of the most

---

The March of the Empires

First: Assyria
Second: Babylonia
Third: Persia

---

enlightened rulers who ever lived. He was a liberator more than a conqueror. The Cyrus Cylinder, an existing barrel-shaped clay form made at the time of Cyrus, tells that Cyrus captured Babylon without a battle. People stood along the streets shouting welcome to him. The cylinder also says that Cyrus allowed captives to return to their homelands and rebuild their temples.

Because Cyrus had released the Jews before the Chronicler began writing, the Chronicler was able to write from the viewpoint of freedom and what that freedom meant. His one central conviction was that the Jews were called to be a church, a worshiping community, and their personal lives a divine service. For that reason 1 and 2 Chronicles is a theological account. It is history but not history in the general sense. It is history interpreted in the light of the purpose of God's people; they are to be a beacon to the nations.

In recording the history of the Jews the Chronicler emphasized the history of Judah rather than Israel and Judah. Also the focus is upon the religious development rather than political events. Special stress is on the priests, the care of the Temple, and the religious music.

The people of Israel had disappeared as a distinct group. Only a remnant of the people of Judah had survived. It was on them that the responsibility of passing along their religious heritage rested. When Cyrus freed them, it was as though they had been given a new beginning, yet that beginning was intimately entwined with the past. With the freedom offered to them by Cyrus they could return to Jerusalem, rebuild the house of the Lord, and become the people they were destined to become.

Ezra

Ezra and Nehemiah, like 1 and 2 Chronicles, were originally one book. They are a continuation of 1 and 2 Chronicles, and they were probably written by the same author. The writing is from the same viewpoint—that the Jews were a people covenanted to God and that their history and future were entwined.

The Book of Ezra is named for a Jewish priest who is introduced midway through the book. The first verses in Ezra are identical to the last ones in 2 Chronicles, a repetition that probably served to show that the Ezra-Nehemiah scroll directly followed the 1—2 Chronicles scroll. The book then takes up the account of the Jews after they were freed by Cyrus. It tells about the Jews who accepted the opportunity offered by Cyrus to return to Jerusalem and what they encountered when they got there.

Not many Jews were anxious to go to Jerusalem; they had been in Babylon so long that Babylon seemed like home. The first group that assembled to make the trip came from mixed backgrounds. Some could trace their ancestry back to the Jews of Judah, and some couldn't. They went back, however, not as a nation but as a people bound together for a common cause, that of establishing a religious community and of returning to the faith of the Jewish fathers. They knew they were still under the authority of Persia, yet they could exercise freedom of religion.

When they reached Jerusalem, the group found a confusing mass of debris and weeds; war and decades of neglect had ravaged the Holy City. Producing order from the chaos was a slow dismal process. It was not until the second year in Jerusalem that they began building the foundation of the Temple. After the foundation was completed, the Temple proper was not constructed until some years later because of trouble with neighboring countries.

The neighbors who caused the most trouble were the Samaritans, descendants of people who had been placed in the vicinity of Samaria, by the Assyrians. The Samaritans felt kinship to the Jews because some of them had Israelite blood, and nearly all of them were familiar with the Jewish religion. They offered to help build the Temple. Whether or not their offer was sincere is uncertain, but the offer was refused, and a prolonged feud began between the Jews and the Samaritans. (The feud continued throughout the remainder of the Bible. At Mount Gerizim the Samaritans built a rival temple of their own; see discussion of Mount Gerizim in the Deuteronomy section of this book.)

The Temple the Jews built became known as the second Temple or Zerubbabel's Temple. Zerubbabel served as governor of Jerusalem while the Temple was being constructed. He was a descendant of Jehoiachin, one of the last kings of Judah and the one who had been taken to Babylon as a prisoner (see 2 Kings 24:11-12; 25:27-30). The Temple was about the size of Solomon's Temple but lacked its grandeur.

From time to time following the decree of freedom issued by Cyrus, additional groups of people left Babylon for Jerusalem. One group was led by the priest, Ezra.

Ezra was probably more learned in the Jewish Scriptures than any other scholar then living. He was especially familiar with the laws of Moses, and he was anxious that Jews begin to obey those laws. He was convinced that all the troubles his people had experienced over the years could be directly traced to their failure to obey the laws. He was particularly interested in the laws concerning marriage. Moses said that the Israelites should not intermarry with other people because of the perverted religions of other peoples. Yet they had not obeyed. Even Solomon had married foreigners and had built temples to gods and goddesses. Ezra did not want the same mistake repeated.

God had preserved a remnant of his people. That remnant had returned to Jerusalem and had an opportunity to make a new beginning. The one essential in beginning again was that the religion be kept pure. To Ezra the only way to keep the religion pure was to keep the race pure. For that reason he wanted Jews to avoid intermarriage with foreigners at all costs.

To his horror Ezra discovered that some Jews had married foreigners. He became distraught, tore his clothes, pulled his hair from his head, and fell down before the Temple sobbing and praying. Crowds gathered, sympathizing, and crying with him.

Because of Ezra the people of Jerusalem were overwhelmingly in favor of forbidding Jews to marry non-Jews. All Jews who had married outside the race were compelled to divorce immediately. All foreign mates and their children had to leave the country.

(Because of his efforts to promote a religion based on the laws of Moses Ezra has sometimes been called "the father of Judaism." Not all Jews of Ezra's day, however, believed in the strict racial purity that Ezra promoted. They felt that God had chosen their ancestors not for racial exclusionism but for sharing their faith. Many scholars believe that the two little books, Ruth and Jonah, became popular at the time of Ezra. Ruth showed that the great king David descended from a foreign Moabite woman. And Jonah showed that God cared about the Ninevites even though they were not only foreigners but were enemies of the Jews.)

Nehemiah

Nehemiah was a Jew who lived at the same time as Ezra. In the effect he produced, Nehemiah was as identical to Ezra as a second sleeve cut for the same coat. He believed as Ezra, was as strong willed as Ezra, and was as influential as Ezra.

Nehemiah worked in the palace of Artaxerxes, the king who ruled the Persian Empire from about 465 to 424 BC. Twice the king granted him leaves and appointed him during those times as governor of Jerusalem. During his first term as governor, he led the Jews to rebuild the city walls that had been in ruins since the Babylonian War. During his second term, he reduced taxes and mortgage interest rates, created support for the priests so they could perform religious duties rather than having to do secular work to support themselves, and made the sabbath day one of rest instead of a business day.

Like Ezra, Nehemiah insisted that the Jews separate themselves from all other peoples. Once when he chanced to hear some children speaking a foreign language and realized that they were half Jewish and half foreign he became so angry that he beat their fathers (Neh. 13:23-27). But he also reasoned with them, explaining how in the past faithful people had turned from God because of being married to people who did not know God.

Ezra was a priest in Jerusalem at the same time that Nehemiah was governor. Both men worked to reestablish the Levitical priesthood, the religious holidays, and to teach the Jews their history.

Esther

The Book of Esther is named for the main character in the book, a beautiful Jewish girl who became queen of Persia. The book is a dramatic account of a plot to annihilate the Jews, a plot that failed because Esther risked her life to save her people.

The account is written like a novel; the reader is kept in suspense as the story grows in complexity. The scene is Susa, the winter capital of the Persian kings. The time is during the reign of Ahasuerus who reigned from 485 to 465 BC.

Besides Esther and her husband, King Ahasuerus, the two chief personalities in the book are Mordecai, Esther's cousin who had adopted her and raised her, and Haman, the highest official in the king's court. The plot centers around Haman's fury at Mordecai who refused to bow to him. Because of his hatred for Mordecai, Haman began hating all Jews. He had a gallows built and developed a scheme for hanging Mordecai and also a plan for exterminating all other Jews on a day that was chosen by lot. Esther learned of the scheme and through a series of developments turned the scheme so that Haman died on the gallows intended for Mordecai and the slaughter of the Jews was averted.

The Book of Esther holds a unique place among the Old Testament books not only because of the way it is written and what it says but because of what it has meant to the Jewish people from the time of its writing to the modern day. It is a book of deliverance. In the Book of Exodus the Israelites were delivered from slavery. In the Book of Esther descendants of those original slaves were delivered from destruction.

In commemoration of the events told about in Esther a new Jewish religious festival was established—the Feast of Purim. *Pur* means lot, the manner Haman used for determining the day the Jews were to be slaughtered. Purim is the only Jewish religious holiday that is not a serious holy day but is entirely a day of fun. It is celebrated with eating and drinking, with laughter and masquerades, with the hanging of Haman in effigy. It is, above all, a children's day. Children go to the synagogue in a carnival mood, carrying noisemakers in their hands. A reader begins reading aloud the Book of Esther. The children sit poised and ready. At the first mention of Haman's name they erupt, stamping, hissing, and shaking their noisemakers. The crescendo builds as Haman's name is repeated throughout the reading. For the children it is a day of unrepressed excitement. For adults it is a day of encouragement, a day of being glad over the continued existence of the Jews.

Daily Bible Reading Schedule

Week 14
Ezra 1:1-11
Ezra 3:10 to 4:5
Ezra 5:1-17
Ezra 6:1-5,13-16
Ezra 7:1-10; 8:35 to 9:3
Ezra 9:5-15
Ezra 10:1-17

Week 15
Neh. 1:1-11
Neh. 2:1-20
Neh. 4:1-6; 6:15-16
Neh. 5:1-19
Neh. 8:1-3,13-18
Neh. 13:1-14
Neh. 13:15-30

Week 16
Esther 1:1 to 2:11
Esther 2:12 to 3:15
Esther 4:1-17
Esther 5:1-14
Esther 6:1-7,10
Esther 8:1-17
Esther 9:1 to 10:3

Suggested Topics for Further Research

Persian Empire: nation that freed the Jews from Babylon
Media: nation that merged with Persia to form Persian Empire
Cyrus the Great: king of Persia (see Cyrus Cylinder; Tomb of Cyrus)
Persepolis: a capital of Persia
Susa: a capital of Persia
Marathon, battle of: battle between Persians and Greeks
Xerxes: king of Persia, probably same as Ahasuerus, husband of Esther
Darius: king of Persia who failed in an attempt to conquer Greece
Purim: religious festival based on Book of Esther

Reinforce Your Memory

First and 2 Chronicles give, to a large extent, the same record that is in the books of _____ and _____ although the emphasis is on _____, not on Israel and Judah.

Second Chronicles gives one vital new piece of information that is not given in Kings. It is that the Jews were freed by _____, ruler of the _____ _____. The writer wrote from the viewpoint of freedom and what that freedom meant therefore the focus is on _____ development rather than political events.

Ezra gives an account of the first Jews who returned and of the building of the _____ which was called _____ _____ or the _____ _____.

Nehemiah was governor of Jerusalem and directed the rebuilding of the city's _____. He and Ezra both worked to reestablish the _____ of Moses.

The Book of Esther is an account of an _____ to annihilate the Jews.

Draw a timeline and mark on it the date Cyrus freed the Jews.

In the space below draw a map showing the outline of the Persian Empire.

SECTION 3

Literature of the Old Testament

With Esther the connected historical account in the Old Testament comes to a close. The story of the Jews does not stop of course, but the part of their history that is recorded in the Old Testament does. (Daniel tells of later history, but it is not presented in the same way that earlier Old Testament books present history.)

The remaining twenty-two books in the Old Testament contain religious writings of varied kinds: songs, poetry, proverbs, sermons, exhortations, and some

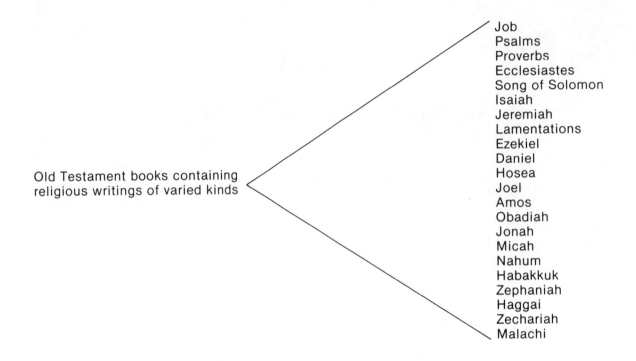

Old Testament books containing religious writings of varied kinds

Job
Psalms
Proverbs
Ecclesiastes
Song of Solomon
Isaiah
Jeremiah
Lamentations
Ezekiel
Daniel
Hosea
Joel
Amos
Obadiah
Jonah
Micah
Nahum
Habakkuk
Zephaniah
Haggai
Zechariah
Malachi

facts about some of the people who spoke or wrote some of the words. Many of the books were written by and for people told about in the Books of Samuel, Kings, Ezra, and Nehemiah.

It is through the literature that the reader of the Bible catches the real majesty of biblical writings. In the literature the writers confess all facets of their thoughts, longings, and hopes. At times they express deep despair; at others they are as free souls, soaring unbridled through limitless spaces of delight.

The books containing the literature fall into three general categories. One is Wisdom Literature: Job, Proverbs, and Ecclesiastes belong in this category. Another type is song: Psalms and the Song of Solomon are collections of songs. The third and largest category is classed as prophetic writings: fifteen of the last seventeen books in the Old Testament, all but Lamentations and Daniel, belong here.

Wisdom Literature

Wisdom Literature comes from the teachings of the wise. For religious education the ancient Hebrews relied not only on the priests and prophets but on the wise men and women. Wisdom teachers were linked to God just as were the priests and prophets, yet what they said did not fall into the same confines.

The priests taught the written law. They reminded the people of God's acts in history, they led religious festivals, they cared for the Temple. The prophets, in contrast, had current messages that burned inside them until they spilled over, messages that fitted particular times and particular situations.

Wisdom teachers did not concern themselves with institutional religion like the priests; instead they stirred up the minds of people concerning the workaday world. They did not stress God's attitude toward the behavior of mankind, as did the prophets; instead they motivated people to use intelligence in recognizing sensible ways of life. Intelligence, however, was not seen as a separate entity but as God-given ability that could be cultivated through study and training. Skill came first of all from God, second from training, and third, from experience.

Wisdom, as possessed by the wisdom teachers, corresponds only in part to what we usually think of today as wisdom. To have wisdom was to have more than knowledge; it was to have moral discernment, to know the proper, the good thing to do. To be wise was the opposite of being a fool. The fool was seen as stupid, quarrelsome, immoral, headstrong, lazy. The wise person was seen as self-controlled, diligent, upright, honest, kind, gifted. Right was the way of wisdom; wrong the way of folly.

Wisdom leaders centered their advice on practical matter-of-fact knowledge that enabled a person to turn from folly to sensibleness. They delved deeply into human problems, analyzing, probing, poring over anguishing experiences. They were keen observers who often looked at nature—the bird, the tree, the ant—for lessons on the way of life, the meaning of life.

Wisdom leaders taught from experience that wisdom is a gift of God, not human achievement. When confronted with things "too wonderful" to understand, like "the way of an eagle in the sky" (Prov. 30:18-19), they felt awe rather than frustration. They were not defeated by what they did not know but lifted to a higher plateau as they considered the unfathomableness of their Creator.

Songs of Israel

Biblical people were rarely unresponsive, silent people. They related to events and expressed their reactions to events. They praised God for blessings, complained to him when they had troubles, questioned him when they did not understand. All these feelings they expressed in their songs.

The songs recorded in the Bible reflect a long history of individual and community worship. (Songs are found throughout the Bible, not just in the literature section.) Most of them are either hymns of praise or hymns of petition.

The praise hymns express joy and thanksgiving, appreciation for the law and for God's care, and they marvel at the infinite magnitude of God. They were raised with a hope based on what had happened in years gone by—an acknowledgment that God had heard prayers in the past and had answered them, therefore prayers in the present could be subject to the same omnipotent attention.

The hymns of petition were raised with requests for help with difficulties, revenge over an enemy, clarity of understanding. They were lifted to an ear that hears, with the knowledge that God is ever present, and that he does care.

Prophetic Writings

The books classed as prophetic writings contain messages spoken by some of the most disturbing men who ever lived. They were called prophets. What was so different about them, and what was the substance of their messages?

A prophet is generally thought of as a "foreteller," yet that word does not accurately describe the biblical prophet. Biblical prophets made predictions about the future, but most often they spoke about the future for the express purpose of changing the way people acted in the present. A disaster predicted was not a disaster inevitable but a disaster avoidable, *if* people would change their wicked ways. God warned people through the prophets, giving them a chance to turn from the kind of life that invited catastrophe. As Jeremiah said of God, "If at any time I declare concerning a nation or a kingdom, that I will . . . destroy it, and if that nation . . . turns from its evil, I will repent of [turn from] the evil I intended to do to it" (Jer. 18:7-8).

The prophets weren't philosophers who spoke only of the nature of God or of humankind but were individuals who *experienced* God. They perceived his inner tension, his anger, his anxiety. They knew the double anguish God endures when one person injures or mistreats another. With God they longed to rescue the one who was suffering and at the same time alter the behavior of the one who was causing the suffering.

The task of the prophet was not easy. He was often ridiculed and scorned. People accused him of being an enemy of the king and the nation. Yet he spoke as he did because he could not stay silent when he saw men and women being callous toward God and toward their fellow human beings.

Some of the writing in the prophetic books is melodious and descriptive of the beauty of nature, yet the prophets were not intent on turning catchy phrases but on helping people see themselves in relation to God. They all had one major subject—the behavior of society, the moral conduct of people. Their concern was with the plight of orphans and widows, the poor and mistreated. To them indifference to the needs of people was a malignancy in the lungs of the nation; injustice was a plague of locusts devastating the fields; cheating was inviting the sky to fall; greed was suicide for the inhabitants.

The prophets were intent on wrenching consciences; their phrases were designed to shock. Their words were like fire; they burned. They criticized the mockery that had characterized the lives of the rich—those who carefully observed religious ceremonies while in their minds they were wishing the services were over, so they could get back to mixing trash with wheat and selling it to the poor.

To the prophets a single act of cheating or of injustice was a threat to the earth's existence; no deed that had anything to do with good or evil was slight or minor. Charitable wrappings could not hide cruelty, nor could a benevolent song soften brutality. Behavior affected the cosmos.

But the prophet was not always understood. People heard his rage, but they could not always comprehend his outrage.

Nearly all the prophets whose writing is included in the literature section of the Bible were born and died during the period of time between 800 and 400 BC. A few of them came from families of influential position (Isaiah was probably related to the royal family; Jeremiah and Ezekiel were from the priestly tribe), but many came from the ordinary strata of society. To understand the prophets, the reader must gain some insight into the situation in which the prophets lived and to whom they spoke. They were people of their times, and what they said was specifically addressed to people of their own day.

In ancient times the writings of the biblical prophets were grouped together in four scrolls. One contained the Book of Isaiah. A second contained the Book of Jeremiah. The third contained the Book of Ezekiel. The fourth, called the Book of the Twelve, contained the twelve short Books of Hosea, Joel, Amos, Obadiah, Jonah, Micah, Nahum, Habakkuk, Zephaniah, Haggai, Zechariah, and Malachi.

The scrolls were all anthologies. The word *anthology* comes from two Greek words: *anthos* which means flower and *legein* which means to pick. The four anthologies—Isaiah, Jeremiah, Ezekiel, and the Twelve—are like four bouquets of flowers that have been carefully picked yet casually arranged. It is as though each was a vase containing mixtures of daisies and roses, violets and gladioli, zinnias and marigolds—all grouped together in an informal arrangement. In the four anthologies poems and prose, speeches and biographical information, historical data, and joys and sorrows are all massed, not separated according to date or form. For that reason the books of the prophets can seem confusing to the casual reader, yet study can make the student feel like a bee that has discovered an orchard in bloom. He or she has found food that can satisfy and be stored for continual use.

Chart 14.
Job through Song of Solomon

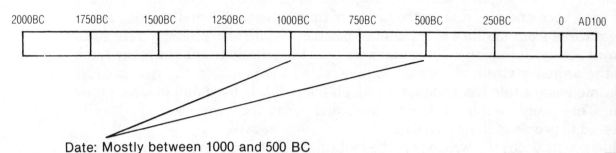

2000BC 1750BC 1500BC 1250BC 1000BC 750BC 500BC 250BC 0 AD100

Date: Mostly between 1000 and 500 BC

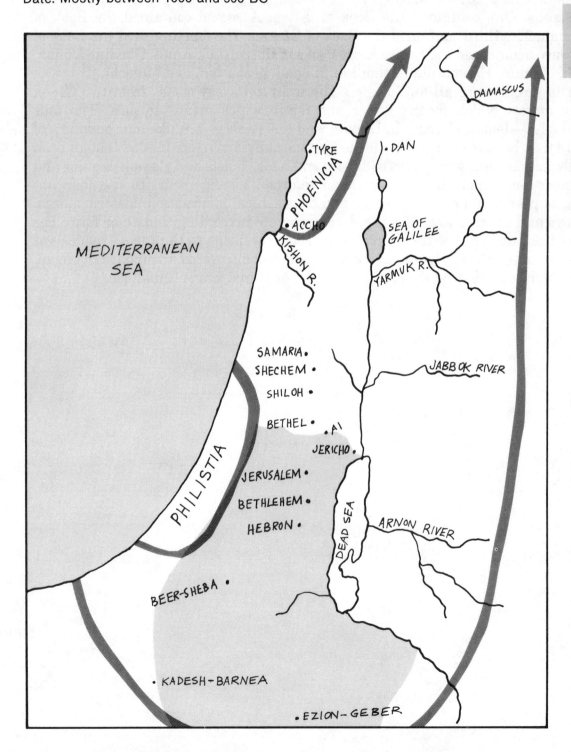

Genesis
Exodus
Leviticus
Numbers
Deuteronomy
Joshua
Judges
Ruth
1 Samuel
2 Samuel
1 Kings
2 Kings
1 Chronicles
2 Chronicles
Ezra
Nehemiah
Esther
Job
Psalms
Proverbs
Ecclesiastes
Song of Solomon
Isaiah
Jeremiah
Lamentations
Ezekiel
Daniel
Hosea
Joel
Amos
Obadiah
Jonah
Micah
Nahum
Habakkuk
Zephaniah
Haggai
Zechariah
Malachi

Matthew
Mark
Luke
John
Acts
Romans
1 Corinthians
2 Corinthians
Galatians
Ephesians
Philippians
Colossians
1 Thessalonians
2 Thessalonians
1 Timothy
2 Timothy
Titus
Philemon
Hebrews
James
1 Peter
2 Peter
1 John
2 John
3 John
Jude
Revelation

Job

The Book of Job is a drama. The introduction and ending are in prose and the main body of the book in poetry. The poetry section is so beautifully written that it has been called the greatest poem of either ancient or modern times.

A definite date and a definite location are unimportant to the meaning of the book because the drama concerns a situation that could have taken place anywhere at anytime. It has to do with personhood, with a single individual being led to discover the difference in hearing about God and in knowing God.

The book is named for Job, a very good and very rich man who suddenly lost everything he possessed—his children, health, wealth, even the respect people had once paid him. Because Job was so good and his suffering so accute, people who know little about the book think it deals with the question, "Why do the good suffer?" Too, the proverbial phrase "patience of Job" has caused people to think Job was a humble individual who endured his sufferings without complaining. Although the mystery of human pain is discussed in the book, that is not the main point of the writing. And Job was an intensely impatient individual who complained bitterly. It is through his thoughts, questions, and debates with others that the actual point of book is reached. That point—the difference between superficial and real faith—does not become clear until the final chapter.

There are only seven speakers in the drama: God, Satan, Job, Eliphaz, Bildad, Zophar, and Elihu. In the book Satan is not the character of evil usually associated with the name but a sort of inspector who checked up on the behavior of people and reported back to God. Eliphaz, Bildad, and Zophar were friends of Job who came to comfort him but accused him of so many wrongs that Job called them "miserable comforters" (Job 16:2). Elihu was a young man who expressed his opinion about Job's problems and about what Job and his friends said to each other.

The poetry in the book is arranged in conversational form, but each speech is longer than that in normal conversation. Job's speeches show his anger at God for allowing so many tragedies to come upon him undeservedly. He even accused God of using him for target practice (Job 16:6-14). The friends' speeches show their shock at Job's arrogance for daring to speak of God as he does. They also show that their religion was based on the belief that the good are always blessed, and the bad always suffer. Job's religion too was based on that theory until his misfortunes had proved it inaccurate.

Finally God spoke to Job. He did not answer Job's questions but directed questions to Job, asking him such things as who decided what size the earth should be, where light originated, and who gave the horse his might. As he listened, Job realized he had been talking as if he knew how to run the world. He suddenly saw himself as he really was—a man in need of help with his problems. In humble recognition of God he apologized: "I have uttered what I did not understand,/things too wonderful for me, which I did not known./. . . I had heard of thee by the hearing of the ear,/but now my eye sees thee" (Job 42:3,5).

Though the book concludes with Job again acquiring health, wealth, family, and prestige, the conclusion is anticlimactic. Inward wealth had already been achieved.

Psalms

The word *psalm* means "religious song." The Book of Psalms is the hymnbook of ancient Israel. It contains 150 songs of varying lengths and kinds. There are hymns of praise, prayers of petition, songs sung at a king's coronation, songs that review God's acts in history. The author of many of the songs is uncertain. Some were written many years before others.

The songs in Psalms are arranged as five different collections of hymns, each group ending with a concluding doxology. In some cases the same psalm, or part of one, appears in more than one of the five collections. (Compare Ps. 14 with Ps. 53; Ps. 40:13-17 with Ps. 70.) The five collections are as follows:

1. Psalms 1-41
2. Psalms 42-72
3. Psalms 73-89
4. Psalms 90-106
5. Psalms 107-150

Unlike English poetry which depends on rhyme or on rhythm of sound with words arranged in a metered form, Hebrew poetry depends on rhythm of thought. Key words are emphasized so that the meaning of a line stands out. Often the lines are arranged so that the second line repeats the thought of the first line; or, occasionally, the second line agrees with the first line by making a reverse statement. Examples of the form, which has come to be called "parallelism," are as follows:

Deliver me from my enemies, O my God,
    protect me from those who rise up against me (Ps. 59:1).

The righteous shall be preserved for ever,
    but the children of the wicked shall be cut off (Ps. 37:28).

A few psalms are arranged in alphabetical order with one, two, or more lines beginning with each of the twenty-two Hebrew letters. Called acrostic structure, the alphabetical use is thought to have been developed by teachers to help pupils memorize more easily. (Psalm 119, the longest chapter in the Bible, is an acrostic poem with eight-line stanzas, beginning with each of the Hebrew letters.)

No other Old Testament book has exercised quite the same function in churches as has the Book of Psalms. It is different from most other Old Testament books in that it is not a book of history or law, but a book of worship. Because most of the songs are relatively short and the contents of individual psalms appeal to the heart, they have been read and sung at worship services in modern times as well as in ancient times. Too, they appeal to individuals for use as private devotions.

Another reason the Book of Psalms is different from other Old Testament books (there are psalms in several Old Testament books, but the Book of Psalms is the only collection of hymns in the Bible) is that in most of the Old Testament the words are addressed to people. In the Psalms people addressed God.

The psalms praise God, and tell why. They complain about problems, and list them. They express religious conflicts, asking why good people suffer and wicked people prosper. The questions are asked with freedom and openness. All things that concern life are brought before God. Nothing is held back, nor is there any pretense. The words express joy, pain, sorrow, sin, excuses, anguish, longings. And they are addressed with the positive conclusion that God is, God hears, God cares, God acts.

Proverbs

The English word *proverb,* which refers to a concise expressive way of stating a general truth, is a title that accurately describes most of the Book of Proverbs. However, the book is actually an anthology containing other forms of composition as well as pithy sayings. In several instances there are rather long descriptions (chapter 7 describes a bad woman, chapter 31 an excellent one). In other places several verses all relate to one subject, yet most of the book is made up of statements that take no more than two lines before turning to a different subject. The statements are not ones that just happened to become popular over a period of time but were carefully composed by thinkers who were spoken of as "the wise." For that reason Proverbs is one of the biblical books belonging to the category of Wisdom Literature.

Although the Wisdom writers gave practical advice about daily life rather than taught scriptural law, as did the priests, or preached specific messages from God, as did the prophets, their advice was not just secular. Its foundation was in God: "The fear of the Lord is the beginning of knowledge" (Prov. 1:7). The wisdom they taught involved a union of intelligence and morality. Wisdom was seen as the art of living well.

The teaching in Proverbs is most often presented through contrasts—the virtuous woman *versus* the immoral woman; the industrious worker *versus* the slothful; the one who accepts instruction *versus* the scoffer. The contrast used is not of intelligence compared with stupidity but of wisdom compared with folly. A wise person had gifts (talents, ability), and those gifts were developed into morally upright skills; a foolish person might also have possessed gifts but indulged in destructive habits. The Book of Proverbs teaches standards of behavior: respect for women, marriage faithfulness, obedient children, honesty, considerateness, reverence for God. It warns against pitfalls: drunkenness, laziness, robbing, oppressing, getting involved with wrong influences. It shows that wisdom involves doing right as well as using good sense; choosing right over wrong makes intelligence worthwhile.

The Book of Proverbs is made up of several collections of writings. The major collections are:

1. Proverbs 1—9
2. Proverbs 10—22:16
3. Proverbs 22:17—24
4. Proverbs 25—29
5. Proverbs 30—31

At least two of the collections (the second and fourth) are attributed to Solomon. He is credited with having written 3000 proverbs and 1005 songs (1 Kings 4:32) in his lifetime, and it is possible that he wrote, or collected, much of the material in Proverbs. From the style of writing, scholars believe some parts of the book came from a time earlier than Solomon. Other parts came from the period after the Jews had returned to Jerusalem after spending more than half a century in Babylon. One section of the book is made up of a collection made during the reign of Hezekiah. (See Prov. 25:1.)

The writers of Proverbs were keen observers of the world around them. They drew insights from what they saw (even the ant), from experiences, and from the writings of people who had lived before them. In their writings they focused not on nations or the movement of history, but on individuals who could have lived at any time. In most instances they dealt with unglamorous, ordinary problems ranging from overeating to nagging, from temper to idleness.

Ecclesiastes

The title *Ecclesiastes* is not a person's name but refers to one speaking before an assembly. The book is written in the form of a lecture that could have been presented before an audience. It is not a sermon but a searching probe of an intelligent mind raising doubts and questions about the meaning of life. The writing is melodious, particularly the most familiar portion of the book—the section on time found in 3:1-9. It is also melancholy, setting a tone different from other Old Testament books. The topics expressed are so interwoven that the thoughts are not easy to follow, and the book must be read with care for its meaning to become clear.

The writing falls into the category of Wisdom Literature and clearly demonstrates just what the biblical view of wisdom is. It shows that human wisdom cannot give ultimate answers, but that humans should ask questions and seek as much information as possible. What others have learned and passed along is motivating, "The sayings of the wise are like goads" (12:11), and "wisdom helps one to succeed" (10:10), leading a person to sharpen an ax rather than exert the energy required to cut with a dull one.

The writer of Ecclesiastes encouraged study, the use of common sense, and the application of the mind to problems. "The advantage of knowledge is that wisdom preserves the life of him who has it" (7:12), he said. He used the example of a poor wise man who, by his wisdom, saved a city. No one remembered the man's name; he didn't become famous like those who win battles, yet "Wisdom is better than weapons of war" (9:18).

Because the Book of Ecclesiastes seems pessimistic and mentions that "there is nothing better for a man than that he should eat and drink, and find enjoyment in his toil" (2:24), some have likened the writer to those who adopted an "eat, drink, and be merry" philosophy. Yet he was teaching that satisfaction is not found in gaining great wealth, in becoming a hero, or in gaining fame. If people have their needs supplied, and have challenging and fulfilling work to do, there is nothing better to be had. Yet even that does not give satisfaction. Satisfaction comes from recognizing that God has provided the food and the opportunity. It is a right relationship with God that gives joy: "For apart from him who can eat or who can have enjoyment?" (2:25).

Song of Solomon

The Song of Solomon is a short book containing romantic songs dealing with love and courtship. There is no obvious reason for the book having Solomon's name in its title although he may have written some of it, or it may have been written during his lifetime.

The book is totally unlike any other in the Old Testament and no other has been interpreted in so many different ways. God's name is not mentioned in it, making it the only other book besides Esther that does not specifically mention God.

Most scholars believe Song of Solomon was written by several people rather than one. The unity of the book comes from the single theme that runs through it. It is a poem in praise of love, and speaks of the devotion of a man and woman for each other.

Because the songs deal with love and courtship, many have interpreted the book as an allegory, symbolizing the love God has for people. Christians have sometimes interpreted it as Christ's love for the church. Another interpretation is that the book is a play with the songs used as dialogue. This view involves several characters, the main one being a beautiful country maiden who was placed in the king's harem. She longed to return home so she could marry a beloved shepherd boy, and when the king learned of her longing, he allowed her to go free.

A number of other interpretations have been presented by different scholars. Some say it is simply a collection of folk songs, others that there is no need at all for a symbolic meaning because throughout the Bible the unity between a man and woman is stressed. Genesis 2:24 says, "A man leaves his father and his mother and cleaves to his wife," and Ephesians 5:28 says, "Husbands should love their wives as their own bodies."

In modern times selections from the book have sometimes been used at Jewish religious ceremonies commemorating the new year or the Day of Atonement. Also the songs are occasionally sung at modern weddings.

Reinforce Your Memory

Job is written as a drama and gives an account of a man who experienced traumatic _____, yet through them grew to understand the difference in hearing about God with the ears and in _____ God personally.

Psalms is the _____ book of ancient Israel. It contains _____ collections of songs.

Proverbs is a book comprised mostly of short _____ that encourage wise moral _____. What are some standards it discusses?

Ecclesiastes is in the form of a _____ presented before an audience. Although the tone of the book is melancholy, the conclusion is that through a right relationship with God persons find _____.

Song of Solomon is a book of _____ poems.

Draw a timeline showing the period in which most biblical poetry was probably written.

Draw a map showing the United Kingdom under David and Solomon as it was likely during their reigns that many psalms and proverbs were written and collected.

Chart 15.
Isaiah through Ezekiel

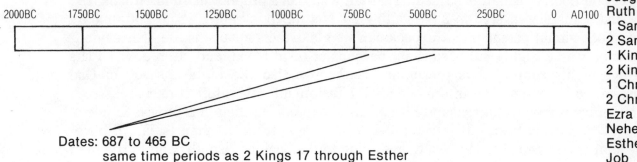

Dates: 687 to 465 BC
        same time periods as 2 Kings 17 through Esther

Genesis
Exodus
Leviticus
Numbers
Deuteronomy
Joshua
Judges
Ruth
1 Samuel
2 Samuel
1 Kings
2 Kings
1 Chronicles
2 Chronicles
Ezra
Nehemiah
Esther
Job
Psalms
Proverbs
Ecclesiastes
Song of Solomon
Isaiah
Jeremiah
Lamentations
Ezekiel
Daniel
Hosea
Joel
Amos
Obadiah
Jonah
Micah
Nahum
Habakkuk
Zephaniah
Haggai
Zechariah
Malachi

Matthew
Mark
Luke
John
Acts
Romans
1 Corinthians
2 Corinthians
Galatians
Ephesians
Philippians
Colossians
1 Thessalonians
2 Thessalonians
1 Timothy
2 Timothy
Titus
Philemon
Hebrews
James
1 Peter
2 Peter
1 John
2 John
3 John
Jude
Revelation

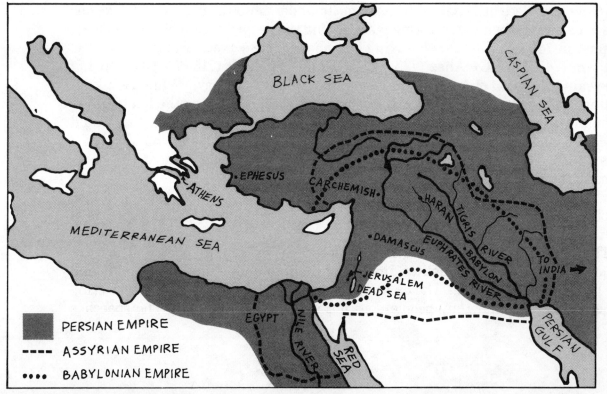

PERSIAN EMPIRE
- - - - ASSYRIAN EMPIRE
•••• BABYLONIAN EMPIRE

Isaiah

The Book of Isaiah is named for a man who was a prophet in Judah during the period of history covered in 2 Kings 15—20. Not much is known about Isaiah; only from occasional passages in the book can we glean facts about his life. It is evident that he was a highly cultured man, perhaps of royal blood, and often advised the kings of his country. His preaching has been called the highest study of God presented by one person in the entire Old Testament. His intellect encompassed a magnificent sweep of ideas, and his genius in expressing them has proved timeless.

The Book of Isaiah, however, must be separated from the man Isaiah. Biblical scholars often separate the two by referring to the book as "Isaiah" and to the man as "Isaiah of Jerusalem." Isaiah of Jerusalem is mentioned only in the first section of the book just as Samuel is mentioned only in the first portion of 1 Samuel.

The chapters in the Book of Isaiah fall into two very distinct parts. Each part is concerned with a totally different period of time. Also there are differences in the style of writing and the subject matter. Because of the differences some scholars speak of the two parts as though they were two separate books, calling them First Isaiah and Second Isaiah. Some scholars divide the book still further calling the final chapters Third Isaiah. Other scholars see the book as entirely from Isaiah of Jerusalem. They explain the differences of the sections in other ways. The use of three divisions makes the book easier to study.

> Part 1: Isaiah 1—39
> Part 2: Isaiah 40—55
> Part 3: Isaiah 56—66

The distinctive characteristics of the three parts are as follows:

Isaiah 1—39 (Sometimes called First Isaiah)

Chapters 1—39 of Isaiah were originally addressed to people who lived at the same time and place as Isaiah of Jerusalem. To understand the chapters the reader needs to be aware of what was taking place among the people. Isaiah was called to be a prophet in 742 BC, the year that King Uzziah died. He served through the reigns of Jotham (742-735 BC), Ahaz (735-715 BC), and Hezekiah (715-687 BC). During those years the nation of Assyria was rising like a giant tidal wave. While Hezekiah was king, the Assyrians swept away the country of Israel, scattering the ten tribes so thoroughly that they never again returned to their homeland. Judah, too, would have fallen had not God miraculously intervened. (Compare Isaiah 36-37 with 2 Kings 18-19). The speeches of Isaiah of Jerusalem were made against the background of the foreboding Assyrian shadow.

The section contains a collection of varied kinds of writing—poetry, songs, parables, history, biography. The arrangement is complicated, and there is a mixture of subjects.

The chapters open with a series of speeches written in poetry. They are emotional appeals to the Israelites, imploring them to understand who God is and what he required of people. "The ox knows its owner,/and the ass its master's crib;/but Israel does not know,/my people does not understand" (Isa. 1:3). The speeches climax with the song of the vineyard, a parable telling what God had done for his people and what he had received in return; he looked for his vineyard "to yield grapes, but it yielded wild grapes" (Isa. 5:2). What could God do? Nothing but trample down the plants and remove them.

Following the poetry is a prose section containing the longest passage in the book about Isaiah himself (Isa. 6). It tells about the experience that led Isaiah to become a prophet and is one of the most moving segments in the entire section. The experience gave Isaiah inspiration to keep preaching even to people who "Hear and hear, but do not understand; see and see, but do not perceive" (Isa. 6:9).

The remaining chapters in the section contain speeches of several kinds interwoven among historical information about King Ahaz and King Hezekiah. Isaiah's rapport with the two kings is an important part of the section. Ahaz was a weak ruler who had, as Isaiah pointed out, an unsure faith which created an insecure throne. He was closed to any suggestions Isaiah made. Hezekiah, in contrast, was a strong leader and a man of faith with whom Isaiah had an excellent relationship.

Part of the speeches interwoven among the historical chapters are oracles, or judgments, against countries and cities around Judah. They tell of some of the evil things done in those places and of God's feelings toward the evils. Other speeches were directed to the people of Judah, and they bring up some of the great themes of the Bible.

One of the themes is that history does not happen by chance; God is in control. Isaiah illustrated God's control by speaking of Assyria's rapid rise in power. An Assyrian king arrogantly boasted, "By the strength of my hand I have done it, and by my wisdom" (Isa. 10:13), but Isaiah pointed out that his boast was like an ax bragging that it controlled the woodsman who cut with it (10:15). God had allowed Assyria to develop and was using the nation as a rod to discipline people who needed correction. Assyria would serve its purpose, then it would be punished for the evil it had done.

Another theme concerns "the remnant" (v. 21). Isaiah explained that because the people had continued "to turn aside the needy from justice and to rob the poor of my people of their right" (Isaiah 10:2), God would punish them. But: "A remnant will return, the remnant of Jacob, to the mighty God" (Isa. 10:21). The doctrine of the remnant was so firmly in Isaiah's mind that he named his first child, "a remnant shall return" (Isa. 7:3).

A third theme, and one of major importance, has been classed as "the messianic hope." Isaiah spoke of a ruler who would appear, one who would not be like rulers before him. He would have wisdom and understanding; he would judge with righteousness.

> And his name will be called
> "Wonderful Counselor, Mighty God,
>   Everlasting Father, Prince of Peace."
> Of the increase of his government and of peace
>   there will be no end (Isa. 9:6-7).

Among other important themes that grew out of Isaiah's ministry was the belief that God would never allow anything to happen to Jerusalem. The city was not destroyed by the Assyrians even though every other country around Judah had suffered the loss of its capital city. The people of Judah became convinced that God would always protect Jerusalem. Although Isaiah said, "Her gates shall lament and mourn; ravaged, she shall sit upon the ground" (Isa. 3:26), and though he warned Hezekiah, "Behold, the days are coming, when all that is in your house, and that which your fathers have stored up till this day, shall be carried to Babylon; nothing shall be left" (Isa. 39:6), the people were certain that the city would remain undamaged. It survived the Assyrian War, and they believed it was because God would not allow his Temple to be destroyed. They believed Jerusalem would always survive.

Isaiah 40—55 (Sometimes called Second Isaiah)

Nearly all of Isaiah 40—55 is written in poetry of exquisite beauty; the author has been called the poet laureate of the Bible. The poetry is filled with joy; it breaks forth like singing. The section begins with the words *Comfort ye* (KJV), and that phrase characterizes the major message.

The words of Isaiah 40—55 are addressed to people who lived approximately 150 years after the people of Isaiah 1—39. The Assyrian Empire had disappeared long before. The Babylonian Empire had come to power, had defeated Judah, and most Jews had been taken as prisoners to Babylon. Years had passed, and the Babylonian Empire had decayed. Cyrus the Great, king of Persia, was about to capture Babylon.

The arrival of Cyrus was good news. He did not treat people as the Assyrians and Babylonians had treated them. His coming brought the hope of freedom. for the Jews it was a happy turning point in their history. The long years of the Exile were over, and a new day was dawning. There was hope of a new exodus. A remnant had survived, and that remnant had a new mission on earth—to become a light to the nations.

The theme "a light to the nations" (42:6) is emphasized through poems about the Servant of the Lord. In Isaiah 40—55 several poems speak of the Servant who had been chosen by the Lord, who had God's Spirit resting upon him, who would bring justice to the earth, and who would cause many nations to see and hear. In contrast to the Servant, a comical description is given of the foolishness of those who turn to idols (Isa. 44:9-20).

The time was important in Jewish history. For years the Jews had been in Babylon where they could have been influenced to worship idols. After all, the idol worshiping Babylonians had won the war. Yet during that time the Jews did not turn to idols but realized their God was not bound to Jerusalem, nor did worship depend on having a temple. Their horizon lifted, and they began to see God in relation to the entire world. Some of them realized God's plan was for the redemption of all mankind. The poems in Isaiah 40—55 show God the Creator as overarching history and as redeemer. They show that a new exodus had been arranged by God, and that the remnant of people who knew about God had been selected for a special task—to dispel darkness so that "all the ends of the earth shall see the salvation of our God" (Isa. 52:10).

Isaiah 56—66 (Sometimes called Third Isaiah)

The final eleven chapters of Isaiah are addressed to the Jews who left Babylon and returned to Jerusalem. They were the remnant that had been freed and had gone to the Holy City to build a new Jerusalem. Times were hard. The Temple that had been burned had to be rebuilt. The city walls that had been knocked down had to be restored. (The time was approximately that of Ezra and Nehemiah.)

The poems of Isaiah 56—66 speak of the sabbath, the Temple, and of keeping God's ordinances as do many other books of the Bible. Yet Isaiah's poems show a new wideness. Keeping the sabbath is shown as keeping the hands from doing evil. God's house as a house of prayer is shown as not just for Jews but for all persons, including foreigners. Keeping a fast is shown not as spreading ashes to show humbleness but through acts of mercy: "Is not this the fast that I choose:/to loose the bonds of wickedness,/to undo the thongs of the yoke,/to let the oppressed go free,/and to break every yoke?/Is it not to share your bread with the hungry, and bring the homeless poor into your house;/when you see the naked, to cover him" (Isa. 58:6-7). The poems are of hope, of looking forward to the future with joy, for God will continue to be with his people.

Jeremiah

Jeremiah was as much a man of his times as any person in the Bible. He was a prophet in Jerusalem from 626 till after 587 BC, a period that grew progressively more difficult with each passing year. The last of those years saw Jerusalem destroyed by the Babylonian army, an event that was the most traumatic the Jews had ever experienced. They didn't believe it could happen; they thought God would never allow it. Jeremiah's work was tied to the fall of Jerusalem, a tragedy that cut like a daggar into his heart.

Very important to the Book of Jeremiah are the kings who ruled Judah just prior to Jerusalem's destruction. The kings were:

Josiah   Ruled 640 to 609 BC: a good king who began a religious reform after discovering the Book of Deuteronomy. Unfortunately his reforms died with him when he was killed in a battle against the Egyptians, and Egypt gained dominance over his country.

Jehoahaz   Ruled 3 months in 609 BC: Josiah's son. Deposed by the Egyptians.

Jehoiakim   Ruled 609 to 598 BC: another of Josiah's sons. Egyptians placed him on the throne with the stipulation that he pay heavy fines to Egypt. He raised the money by taxing his people. Egypt lost dominance because of the rising power of the Babylonian Empire. Jehoiakim agreed to pay fines to Babylon but after three years rebelled. Several countries then attacked Judah and Jehoiakim died, probably in one of the battles. He was a luxury-loving oriental tyrant who helped set his country up for defeat.

Jehoiachin	Ruled 3 months in 598—597 BC: Jehoiakim's son, Josiah's grandson. During his reign Nebuchadnezzar attacked Jerusalem and took everything valuable in the city to Babylon—all gold and silver, every person with strength and ability, and even the king himself.
Zedekiah	Ruled 597 to 587 BC: Jehoiachin's uncle, Josiah's youngest son. Nebuchadnezzar placed him over the few people left in Jerusalem, but even those few rebelled. The rebellion caused Nebuchadnezzar to destroy the city and bring to an end the line of kings from the family of David.

Jeremiah became a prophet in the thirteenth year of the reign of Josiah. Josiah, in the eighteenth year of his reign, began a religious reform; therefore, it must have seemed to Jeremiah that there was hope and that all was going to be well with the small nation of Judah. But under Josiah's successors the country went continually downhill. Jeremiah lived in Jerusalem through those declining years. He stayed there until after Gedaliah, who was appointed governor by the Babylonians after they destroyed the city, was assassinated. The few Jews remaining in Jerusalem then forced him to go with them to Egypt where he probably spent his remaining years.

More is known about Jeremiah than any of the other prophets because the book called by his name tells so much about him. It contains facts about his life as well as sections that have been described as "Jeremiah's confessions" which are words the prophet addressed to God because of the difficulties he had in coping with the way people acted and with the way people treated him.

Jeremiah was the son of a priest from Anathoth, a small town not far north of Jerusalem. He never married and spent all his adult life trying to convince people that God would not continue to bless those who "are skilled in doing evil, but how to do good they know not" (Jer. 4:22). His confessions show the inner tension he was under, the pain and suffering he endured because of how people reacted to what he felt compelled to say.

Other prophets were popular because they said God would always protect Jerusalem. Jeremiah was not popular because he said God would destroy the city because of the evil in it, and if people were to survive they would have to cooperate with the Babylonians. To the people of Jerusalem his words sounded like high treason, and he was looked upon as a traitor.

Jeremiah's basic teaching was similar to that of other prophets: "Thus says the Lord: Do justice and righteousness, and deliver from the hand of the oppressor him who has been robbed. And do no wrong or violence to the alien, the fatherless, and the widow, nor shed innocent blood in this place" (Jer. 22:3). Too, Jeremiah was like a number of the other prophets in that he looked to the day a new kind of king would rule: "Behold, the days are coming, says the Lord, when I will raise up for David a righteous Branch, and he shall reign as king and deal wisely, and shall execute justice and righteousness in the land" (Jer. 23:5). Still, he enjoyed little popularity.

The Book of Jeremiah is not arranged in chronological order but is an anthology made up of four main parts.

1. Jeremiah 1—20: Mostly poetic speeches that plead with listeners to understand themselves and God; some bits about Jeremiah are inserted occasionally
2. Jeremiah 21—45: Information about what Jeremiah did and said
3. Jeremiah 46—51: Mainly poems of judgment against nations near Judah
4. Jeremiah 52: Description of the fall of Jerusalem

Part 1. Jeremiah 1—20.—Chapters 1—20 contain a few facts about Jeremiah's life, but mostly the section consists of Jeremiah's poetic pleas asking the people of Jerusalem to understand themselves and God. Again and again he spoke, telling the people that they had turned from God, and unless they turned back they were going to be punished. "Besiegers come from a distant land; they shout against the cities of Judah. . . . Your ways and your doings have brought this upon you" (Jer. 4:16,18).

To get across his points Jeremiah used a number of visual illustrations. He put a new piece of clothing under a rock where it decayed, then brought it out to show the decay of the people of Jerusalem (Jer. 13:1-11). At another time he crushed a piece of pottery saying Jerusalem would be crushed (Jer. 19:10-11). Because of his words and actions Pashhur, the head priest of the Temple had Jeremiah beaten and put in stocks. In despair he cried out to the Lord: "I have become a laughingstock all the day; everyone mocks me" (Jer. 20:7). He would have liked to stop speaking of the Lord altogether but could not: "If I say, 'I will not mention him,/or speak any more in his name,'/there is in my heart as it were a burning fire/shut up in my bones,/and I am weary with holding it in,/and I cannot" (Jer. 20:9).

Part 2. Jeremiah 21—45.—Chapters 21—45 contain information about Jeremiah and the kings he was associated with. It is not in chronological order, but it is a collection of some writings about some of the more important happenings particularly during the reigns of Jehoiakim and Zedekiah.

Early in Jehoiakim's reign Jeremiah spoke in the Temple saying the Temple would become like Shiloh (a worship center that had disappeared), and the city would become desolate. A crowd gathered, shouting that Jeremiah should be killed for daring to suggest such a thing. King Jehoiakim had already had a prophet killed for saying similar words. (Jehoiakim is the only king of Judah known to have killed a prophet.) Jeremiah escaped death only because years before King Hezekiah had not killed the prophet Micah for saying Jerusalem would be destroyed. Micah's words had made people repent, and Jeremiah spoke for the same purpose: "Amend your ways and your doings, and obey the voice of the Lord your God, and the Lord will repent of the evil which he has pronounced against you" (Jer. 26:13). Ahikam, from one of the most prominent families in Jerusalem, protected Jeremiah, and he was not put to death. People worried little about Micah's or Jeremiah's prediction that Jerusalem would be destroyed. Isaiah, who lived at the time of Micah, had said that it would not, and in Isaiah's lifetime the city had escaped almost certain destruction. They were certain that God would forever shelter the city just as he had during Isaiah's time.

Later in Jehoiakim's reign Jeremiah dictated messages which his secretary Baruch wrote on a scroll and read in the Temple. When government leaders heard the words, they became so alarmed that they arranged for the scroll to be read to the king. Jehoiakim was sitting by an open fire in this winter palace. He listened as three or four columns were read, then cut that portion off with his penknife and threw it into the fire. He repeated the action until the scroll was burned (Jer. 36:1-23). But Jeremiah dictated the words again, plus others. (Much of the Book of Jeremiah probably comes from this dictation to Baruch.)

Jehoiakim's tyrannical rule ended with his death in 598 BC; his son ruled only three months before being captured by Nebuchadnezzar and taken to Babylon, then the last of Judah's kings, the weak Zedekiah took the throne. Zedekiah often asked Jeremiah's advice but was not a strong enough leader to follow Jeremiah's suggestions. Several times Zedekiah put Jeremiah in prison; once he had him thrown into a pit, but each time he allowed the prophet to be rescued.

By the time of Zedekiah's reign the cream of Jerusalem's society had already been taken to Babylon. Jeremiah put on a yoke saying that the remaining people could hope to save their lives only by submitting to the yoke of Babylon. Hananiah, another prophet, broke the yoke saying that God was going to break Babylon, and the people who had been captured would return home within two years. Jeremiah then put on an iron yoke to show that only God could break the yoke of Babylon. He said that Hananiah was making people trust in a lie, and he predicted that Hananiah would die within the year: "In that same year, in the seventh month, the prophet Hananiah died" (Jer. 28:17).

In a vision Jeremiah saw two baskets of figs, one firm and good, the other so bad they couldn't be eaten. The good represented the people who had been taken from Jerusalem to Babylon, the bad represented the city of Jerusalem. Jeremiah saw the hope of the future in those who had been taken to Babylon. He wrote to them telling them to build houses and plant gardens. God would care for them and eventually bring them back to their homeland. They were to begin a new nation and have deeper understanding: "Behold, the days are coming, says the Lord, when I will make a new covenant with the house of Israel and the house of Judah, not like the covenant which I made with their fathers when I took them by the hand to bring them out of the land of Egypt, my covenant which they broke, . . . this is the covenant which I will make. . . . I will put my law within them, and I will write it upon their hearts; and I will be their God, and they shall be my people" (Jer. 31:31-33).

Part 3. Jeremiah 46—51.—The third section of Jeremiah mainly contains poems of judgment against nations and cities from Egypt to Babylon. The poems dramatize the rise of nations and cities and the proud arrogance that leads to downfall. One after another nations sink to rise no more because they oppress, are cruel, and show no mercy.

Part 4. Jeremiah 52.—The book of Jeremiah closes with a description of Babylon's final attack on Jerusalem. Zedekiah, who could have saved himself and the city if he had followed Jeremiah's advice, was forced to watch his sons be killed, then his eyes were put out, and he was put in a Babylonian prison for the remainder of his life.

Jehoiachin, the king who had been taken to Babylon earlier as a prisoner, was eventually freed and given special allowances as a member of royalty. Modern archaeologists have found records listing his name and the daily allowances that were provided for him by the Babylonians.

Lamentations

The Book of Lamentations is a collection of five poems, one poem to each of its five chapters. All five poems are cries over the destruction of Jerusalem. The first four are alphabetical acrostics. The first two chapters each contain one verse beginning with each successive Hebrew letter of the alphabet. Chapter 3 contains three verses for each letter and chapter 4 two verses for each. Although chapter 5 contains a verse for each of the twenty-two letters they are not in alphabetical order like the other chapters.

The poems were probably written shortly after 586 BC, after the Babylonians destroyed Jerusalem. The book is read in Jewish synagogues in memory of that destruction and of the destruction of Jerusalem by the Romans in AD 70.

The poems express the horror of war in all ages. They teach that suffering is the inevitable result of continued sin, that God is righteous in allowing punishment, and that he will help those who trust him.

Ezekiel

Ezekiel, the prophet for whom the Book of Ezekiel is named, lived at the same time as Jeremiah. Like Jeremiah he was deeply affected by the Jerusalem-Babylonian War. He had the same attitude toward the war as Jeremiah, that is that Jerusalem would be destroyed because of her sins and that the Babylonians were God's instruments for the purpose.

Unlike Jeremiah, however, Ezekiel did not live in Jerusalem during the final years before the fall of the city. Ezekiel was captured in the attack that Nebuchadnezzar made on Jerusalem in 597 BC. He was one of the upper class citizens of Jerusalem who, along with their king, Jehoiachin, were taken to Babylon.

In taking the cream of Jerusalem's people to Babylon, Nebuchadnezzar added a talented group to his own city (he utilized their talents), and he also decreased the chance that Jerusalem would rebel against Babylon. But although all the leaders were taken from the city and only the weakest and poorest people left, even those rebelled against Babylon. Eleven years after Ezekiel was captured, Nebuchadnezzar destroyed Jerusalem and put a final end to the rebellions.

The Book of Ezekiel opens about midway between the time that he was captured and the time that Jerusalem was destroyed. Ezekiel had been in Babylon five years and was living in the small town of Tel-abid along with many other Jews. He suddenly had a most peculiar vision. What he saw was so amazing and so unlike anything he had ever seen before that he could describe it only by naming a number of familiar items that it had "the likeness of." It had the likeness of gleaming bronze. It had wheels, wings, and darted with lightning speed. Some part of it reminded him of torches flashing. There was also "the likeness of a throne, in appearance like sapphire; and seated above the likeness of a throne was a likeness as it were a human form" (Ezek. 1:26). The brilliant and overwhelming glow gave "the appearance of the likeness of the glory of the Lord" (Ezek. 1:28). The experience so moved Ezekiel that although he was already a priest he became a prophet. He accepted the task of preaching to the Jewish people whether they heard or refused to hear.

The book begins with an account of the vision of the glory of God then continues with more of Ezekiel's visions and experiences and with the ways he presented God's messages to his people. Often Ezekiel acted out what he wanted to teach. Once he took a brick, drew on it an outline of Jerusalem, then set up around the brick a miniature war scene of tents and weapons to show the situation surrounding Jerusalem. Another time he cut off his hair and divided it into three parts. One part he burned, another he struck with a sword, and the third he scattered to the wind to show that a third of the people of Jerusalem would die of disease and starvation, another third would die in battle, and the remainder would be scattered. People watched Ezekiel, but they were not as interested in the meanings of his acts as they were in the acts themselves. They seemed to think of him as a pantomime artist. Some watched him for amusement; others thought he was weird although they did not seem to become alarmed over his strange behavior. Sometimes in his frustration over their failure to understand, Ezekiel cried out to God, "Ah, Lord God! they are saying of me, 'Is he not a maker of allegories?'" (Ezek. 20:49). Like Jeremiah, he wanted people to understand so badly. He had iron self-discipline and could make himself endure hard and peculiar difficulties. He even suffered the death of his dearly loved wife without showing visible mourning because God had told him to. His strange behavior made people ask questions, and then he was able to speak to them of the God they needed to know.

The book divides easily into three parts. The first part, chapters 1—24, contains prophecies given before the fall of Jerusalem. The second part, chapters 25—33, contains God's judgments against surrounding nations. The final chapters, 33—48, contain prophecies given after the fall of Jerusalem. The entire book covers a period of only about twenty years.

The first section follows the theme of doom. Jerusalem had been evil; Jerusalem was going to fall. A peculiar feature of this section is that Ezekiel was called to be a prophet to the Jews in the country of Babylon, yet his knowledge of what was going on in Jerusalem was so thorough it was almost as if he were hovering over the city looking down on it. Some scholars think he might have visited Jerusalem or that he wrote letters to the people there just as Jeremiah wrote to the people in Babylon. Jerusalem's evil and Jerusalem's downfall constantly dominated Ezekiel's thinking whether he was in Jerusalem or in Babylon.

All that changed after Jerusalem fell. The punishment had arrived, and a new day would follow. Tomorrow could be looked upon with optimism. God's power provided encouragement and comfort; the future could be seen with confidence. Even a valley of dry bones (Ezek. 37) could, with God's Spirit breathing upon them, rise again and live. The Book of Ezekiel ends with detailed data for the construction of a new Temple in Jerusalem. Ezekiel, like Jeremiah, spoke of a new heart, a new spirit, a new covenant, yet he was also very concerned with the forms through which knowledge of God had traditionally been taught. He wanted the sabbath observed. He wanted the Temple restored.

Ezekiel was a strange man as a quick glance at the book will show you. However, a more thorough look gives a different picture. His words and actions show that he used logic, planning, and mental cohesiveness. He was an unusual individual and a brilliant one.

One reason the Book of Ezekiel is different from earlier prophetic books is that Ezekiel cast what he had to say in a different form. That fact illustrates the changing times he was living in. The book marks the transition from the before-the-Babylonian-War period to the after-the-Babylonian-War period. The time was one of dramatic change for the Jewish people. The synagogue (the word means "gathering together"), which later became the place of Jewish religious teaching, was probably coming into being. The Scriptures were being assembled, and their importance recognized. And a new kind of writing, one used by some of the prophets after Ezekiel, was beginning to develop. Called "apocalyptic," the form was a kind of code that utilized strange visions, supernatural scenes, and curious symbolisms. It was usually used during times of persecution when the writer wanted to hide the meaning of what he had to say from persecutors but allow the meaning to be clear to those who understood the code. The fact that Ezekiel mentioned "the likeness of" often in connection with his visions shows that he was familiar with apocalyptic writing and made some use of it.

Apocalyptic writing usually emphasized the coming kingdom of God, the destruction of evil, and the beginning of a reign of peace. Such was Ezekiel's assurance. Even Jerusalem was to have a new name: "The Lord is there" (Ezek. 48:35).

Daniel

The Book of Daniel stands by itself in the Old Testament because it is so different from all other books. It is named for a Jewish man who is traditionally thought of as a prophet, yet he was not at all like other people who are called prophets. He was more like Joseph in the Book of Genesis. Like Joseph he was taken from his native country to a foreign land when he was young. And like Joseph, he rose to a high governmental position in the foreign country.

The twelve chapters in the book fall into two groups of six chapters each. The first six are written in plain storylike fashion. Each chapter gives a record of a different event in the life of Daniel or in the lives of his friends. Each account is an example of people who trusted God in times of crisis and of God's care of them through the crisis. The second six chapters are written in the apocalyptic style of writing (see discussion of apocalyptic writing at end of Ezekiel section of this book), the kind of code sometimes used during times of persecution. The chapters contain descriptions of dreams and visions about historical events.

The events told about in the book cover a long period of time, from around 600 to 164 BC. Daniel is the only book in the Old Testament that reaches so close to the time of the New Testament. The book is not a history, yet to understand what is said it is necessary that the reader be familiar with four important historical periods that took place between 600 and 164 BC.

The first is the period of the Babylonian Empire told about in both 2 Kings 24—

Chart 16.
Daniel

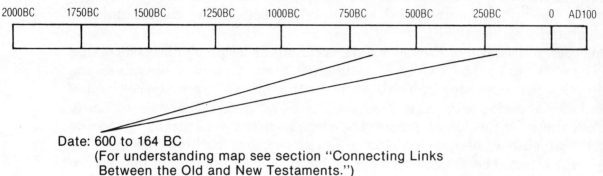

Date: 600 to 164 BC
(For understanding map see section "Connecting Links
Between the Old and New Testaments.")

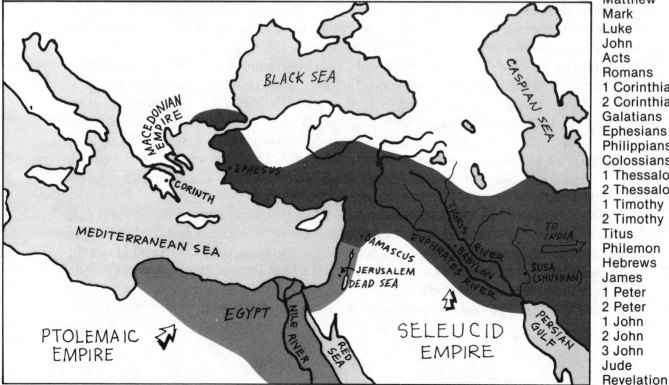

25 and 2 Chronicles 36:5-21. Daniel was a youth when Nebuchadnezzar, king of the Babylonians, attacked Jerusalem, and he was one of a select group of Jews Nebuchadnezzar ordered taken to Babylon for training in Babylonian culture. Daniel was such an outstanding leader and learned so easily that he was appointed to a prominent office in the Babylonian government. In that position, however, he did not give up his Jewish identity or his religion.

The second historical period important to the Book of Daniel is that of the Persian Empire which arose and replaced the Babylonian (see 2 Chron. 36:22-23, Ezra, Nehemiah). The Persians recognized Daniel's ability, and he became a leader among them just as he had been among the Babylonians.

The third historical period important to the Book of Daniel is the Greek. The Greeks are not mentioned much in the Old Testament, yet they exerted a great influence over the Jews toward the time of the New Testament. (For a discussion of the Greek influence see "Connecting Links Between the Testaments" section of this book.)

The fourth historical period was an outgrowth of the Greek period. The Greek nation divided into four parts. A ruler of one of them, Antiochus Epiphanes, caused the Jews great misery. (For a discussion of Antiochus Epiphanes see "Connecting Links Between the Testaments" section of this book.)

Many feel that it is to the people who were suffering under Antiochus Epiphanes that the Book of Daniel is primarily addressed. Others feel that the Book of Daniel was written much earlier. It is a book of encouragement to individuals who were undergoing terrible trials. Daniel and his friends had faced great trials, yet they trusted God and demonstrated faith in such a way that even their persecutors recognized the power of God. The book inspires later generations to do the same.

Daniel teaches faith without arrogance. It teaches that God brings individuals and nations through times and seasons toward an ultimate goal—a kingdom "that shall not be destroyed" (7:14), that will be made up of "the saints of the Most High" (7:18), and will be led by "one like a son of man" (7:13). This kingdom is the goal of history. It is not a political kingdom, nor does it come through human achievement. It is a divine victory and accomplishment.

Daily Bible Reading Schedule

Week 17
Job 1
Job 2:11 to 3:11
Job 8:1-6; 9:1-2,15-20
Job 11:1-6; 12:1-5
Job 15:1-6; 16:1-4
Job 23:1-5; 38:1-13
Job 42

Week 18
Ps. 1
Ps. 26
Ps. 75
Ps. 150
Prov. 1:1-19
Prov. 12:1-15
Prov. 31:10-31

Week 19
Eccl. 1
Eccl. 2
Eccl. 3:1-19
Eccl. 5:11-20
Eccl. 8:16 to 9:6
Eccl. 10:1-10; 12:13
Song of Sol. 4:1-7

Week 20
Isa. 1:1-4,12-17
Isa. 3:8-11,24-26
Isa. 5:1-7,17
Isa. 6:1-13
Isa. 11:1-9
Isa. 44:9-20
Isa. 59:1-2; 61:1-8

Week 21
Jer. 1:1-10
Jer. 7:1-15
Jer. 18:1-12
Jer. 20:7-18
Jer. 28
Jer. 36:1-10,21-26
Jer. 23:5-33

Week 22
Lam. 5
Ezek. 1:28 to 2:7
Ezek. 4:1-3; 5:1-8
Ezek. 11:14-21; 18:1-9
Ezek. 33:23-33
Ezek. 37:1-14
Ezek. 40—48 (scan chapters)

Week 23
Dan. 1:1-17
Dan. 2
Dan. 3
Dan. 6
Dan. 7
Dan. 10
Dan. 11

Suggested Topics for Further Research

Apocalyptic literature: writing with a hidden meaning
Parallelism and strophe: Hebrew poetry forms
Review: Assyrian Empire in association with Isaiah
    Babylonian Empire in association with Jeremiah, Ezekiel, Daniel
    Persian Empire in association with Daniel
Zoroastrianism: a Persian religion

Reinforce Your Memory

The Book of Isaiah is easier to study when divided into three parts. The first part concerns the time that the _____ Empire was in power, the second concerns the time the _____ Empire was in power, and the third concerns the time the _____ Empire was in power.

Jeremiah contains messages spoken by a prophet who lived in Jerusalem during the _____ War.

Lamentations is a collection of _____ poems all dealing with the _____ of war.

Ezekiel contains messages spoken by a Jewish priest to his own people, the _____, while they were in Babylon where they had been taken as _____ _____ _____.

Daniel is a book named for a man who served in governmental positions under both the _____ and the _____.

Draw a timeline and mark on it the approximate dates that the Assyrian, Babylonian, and Persian Empires became important to the Jews.

Draw a map in the space below showing the extent of the Assyrian and Babylonian Empires.

Chart 17.
Hosea through Malachi

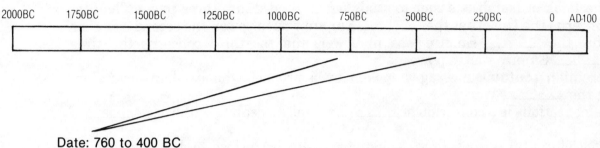

2000BC   1750BC   1500BC   1250BC   1000BC   750BC   500BC   250BC   0   AD·100

Date: 760 to 400 BC

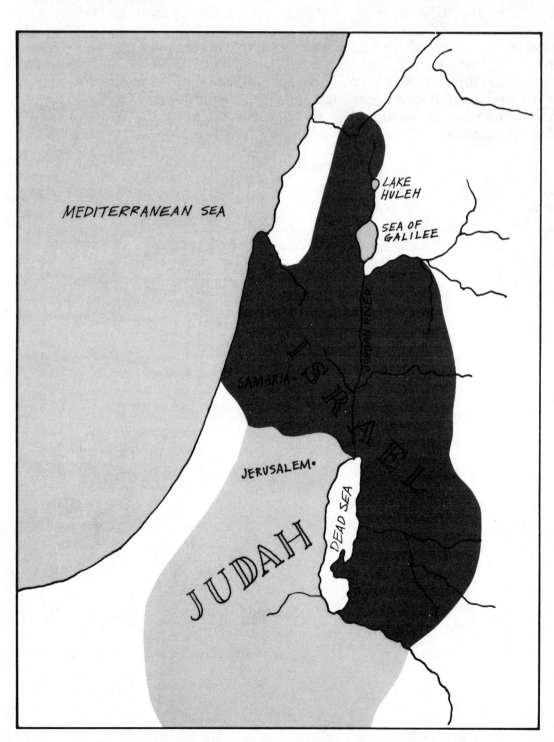

MEDITERRANEAN SEA

LAKE HULEH

SEA OF GALILEE

JORDAN RIVER

SAMARIA

ISRAEL

JERUSALEM

DEAD SEA

JUDAH

Genesis
Exodus
Leviticus
Numbers
Deuteronomy
Joshua
Judges
Ruth
1 Samuel
2 Samuel
1 Kings
2 Kings
1 Chronicles
2 Chronicles
Ezra
Nehemiah
Esther
Job
Psalms
Proverbs
Ecclesiastes
Song of Solomon
Isaiah
Jeremiah
Lamentations
Ezekiel
Daniel
Hosea
Joel
Amos
Obadiah
Jonah
Micah
Nahum
Habakkuk
Zephaniah
Haggai
Zechariah
Malachi

Matthew
Mark
Luke
John
Acts
Romans
1 Corinthians
2 Corinthians
Galatians
Ephesians
Philippians
Colossians
1 Thessalonians
2 Thessalonians
1 Timothy
2 Timothy
Titus
Philemon
Hebrews
James
1 Peter
2 Peter
1 John
2 John
3 John
Jude
Revelation

The Book of the Twelve

The twelve short books from Hosea through Malachi are sometimes called "the minor prophets." The title arose not because the twelve are less important than "the major prophets"—Isaiah, Jeremiah, and Ezekiel—but because the books of the twelve are smaller.

As mentioned in the introduction to Section 3 of this manual, the twelve books once were grouped together in one scroll called "The Book of the Twelve." Together they approximate the size of any one of the major prophets.

The books are not arranged in any particular order. Each one is named for a prophet with the possible exception of Malachi which means "my messenger" and may not be a person's name. The twelve prophets lived at varying times in Israelite history. The earliest probably preached around 760 BC, the latest around 400 BC. Most of them were very affected by their own times, by the king or kings who reigned, and by wars or the threat of wars. For that reason it is important for the reader to become acquainted with the time of the prophet as well as with his message.

Hosea

The Book of Hosea contains messages spoken by a man named Hosea plus some information about his life. He was a native of Israel and preached to his own people. He was a prophet during the final years of the reign of King Jeroboam II and probably for about ten years afterwards, the period of time covered in 2 Kings 14:23-27. The time was difficult both because the kings of Israel were bad and because the nation of Assyria was a constant threat.

Hosea came pleading that the people of Israel recognize their wrongs and change their ways. His was a message of doom. Trouble was inevitable, he said, because of the gross immorality of the people. The behavior he blamed largely on the priests because they had not taught what they were supposed to teach.

The book is in two divisions. Chapters 1—3 tell about Hosea's marriage and the birth of his children. Chapters 4—14 contain messages Hosea delivered to the people of his country. The two parts are dependent upon each other because it was Hosea's experience in marriage that led him to formulate what he taught.

Hosea was married to Gomer, a woman who was unfaithful to him. Repeatedly he tried to win her back from her lovers and to persuade her to live a moral life. Gomer's conduct made her undeserving of love, yet Hosea loved her despite her actions, and he was restless until he brought her back.

Because of his marital difficulties Hosea came to realize that God was experiencing a similar, though much deeper, agony over the behavior of the Israelites. In Gomer's infidelity to him Hosea saw mirrored Israel's unfaithfulness to God (Hos. 9:1-3). In his love for Gomer he saw a reflection of God's love for Israel. In his own forgiveness and efforts to restore Gomer to her place as a faithful wife, he saw a parallel to God's tender mercy (Hos. 14:1-7). If he, an imperfect human being, could love a wife so much even through her infidelity, how much more must the Lord love his sinning people.

Hosea was the first prophet to use the marriage relationship to demonstrate

God's covenant with his people. He saw marriage as a sacred commitment, a contract in which both participants pledged allegiance to each other. The people of Israel had pledged themselves to God, but they had left God for other lovers.

The three chapters that speak of Hosea's marriage are not detailed. Some believe that the marriage was not actual but was used to illustrate Israel's unfaithfulness. The intensity of Hosea's feelings, however, seem to indicate that his marriage experience was real. It is used as a living parable for delivering his messages. His messages in chapters 4—14 are not arranged in any specific order but are often repetitive as he used the same themes when speaking to different groups of people.

Like Jeremiah, who was influenced by him, Hosea was a man of sorrows aching for his people and grasping in his heart some of the pain which he knew God was feeling. He saw God's people not only in the light of a marriage relationship but in a father-son relationship. In the wilderness experience, Israel had been like a trusting child under a father's protective love. Then God had taught Israel, his son, how to walk. But the people had turned from God, therefore a day of judgment was coming. God was going to punish his people in order to teach them. There would be a new wilderness experience, not so God could "get back at them" for their behavior but to bring about redemption and reconciliation.

Hosea's desire was that people would *know* God. He did not mean that the name of God was unknown or even that people did not know how to quote the "Do not kill, do not steal" commandments. He meant that a person who knows God has a perception of rightness in his heart and that perception affects behavior. Kindness and compassion become a way of life. But Israel did not have that understanding. "There is no faithfulness or kindness, and no knowledge of God in the land," he said. "There is swearing, lying, killing, stealing, and committing adultery" (Hos. 4:1-2). He longed for the Israelites to acquire a knowledge of God so that tragedies could be averted—tragedies that inevitably fall upon a people who swear, lie, kill, steal, and commit adultery.

Joel

The Book of Joel is a dramatic poem describing a double catastrophe, a locust plague and a drought. The catastrophe was so devastating that years afterwards fathers told their children about it, and the children told their children.

No definite date of the plague and drought is given although evidences within the book indicate they occurred possibly around 400 BC. At that time the Jews had returned from Babylon after being captive for many years, and they had rebuilt the Temple.

The plague prompted a call for all to gather in prayer. All did gather—old people, children, infants, even brides and grooms (Joel 2:16). The prayer was heard, and the trouble relieved.

The poem then shifts to another theme, the Day of the Lord. Such a day was described as a day of terror for the sinner but of blessing for those who call upon the Lord. (See discussion of Day of the Lord in Zephaniah section of this manual.)

The Book of Joel calls people to alertness and to a recognition of true worship.

"Rend your hearts," the prophet said, "and not your garments" (Joel 2:13).

Amos

The Book of Amos is third in the list of minor prophets, yet he was the first chronologically. He is known as the first of the writing prophets. Other prophets before him, such as Elijah and Elisha, were known mostly through their acts. The messages of Amos were the first to be grouped together and written down in a book named for the prophet who said them.

Amos lived during the time of the Divided Kingdom. He probably preached around 760 BC. At that time Uzziah (also called Azariah) was king of Judah and Jeroboam II was king of Israel. Times were prosperous, although the prosperity was one-sided. The rich were very rich, the poor very poor, and the rich showed no mercy toward the poor.

Amos was from Tekoa, a small town in Judah near Jerusalem, but he preached in Israel where he was treated as an outsider and was resented. He centered his work in Bethel, one of the two cities where Jeroboam I had instituted calf worship. (See 1 Kings 13:26-33.)

The first messages that Amos spoke in Bethel were directed against cities and countries nearby. Each message followed the same basic rhythm: "For three transgressions, . . . and for four, I will not revoke the punishment," meaning that the countries and cities he spoke against had sinned not just once or twice, but repeatedly. For that continued sin God was going to punish them.

The Israelites did not object to Amos speaking about others, but then he began talking about Israel. Israel, he said, was going to be punished worse than the other countries because Israel should have known better.

His words caused Amaziah, priest of Bethel, to send a message to the king saying that Amos was plotting treason. Amos was then ordered to leave the country and to never again appear in Bethel.

Amos defended himself, saying he was not a professional prophet. He was a shepherd and also worked seasonally in the production of sycamore fruit. He had left that work because God had told him to warn the people of Israel.

Amos probably did leave Israel, but he either managed to say what he intended to say before he left or sent his messages to Israel in writing. His words were directed against the wealthy, and his theme was justice. You rich, he said, have winter and summer houses inlaid with ivory. You loll on damask couches, drink wine by the bowlful, and fill your ears with idle music. Your wives are fat as cows and spend their time cursing the poor and demanding of their husbands, "Bring, that we may drink!" (Amos 4:1).

You think you are so good, but your goodness is a farce. God hates your solemn assemblies: he is repulsed by your sacrifices. You make sacrifices only so you can brag; your religious feasts are for show. You think the altar is a bargaining place and that you can placate God by giving gifts. But the noise of your hymns cannot drown the cries of the oppressed. You are not grieved over the sufferings of your fellow citizens.

To Amos justice was the supreme commandment. He didn't define the word, but he made its meaning clear through comparisons. His sermons never displayed a God of miracles; they disclosed the God who cares about how one man treats another.

Obadiah

Obadiah is the shortest book in the Old Testament. It is a poem directed against the Edomites, the descendants of Esau. The theme is the way the Edomites treated their "brother," the descendants of Jacob, Esau's twin. Over and over the poem repeats, "you should not have," as it lists one cruel act after another the Edomites inflicted upon the Israelites—gloating over their troubles, looting their goods, blocking escape routes during war.

Nothing is known about the prophet Obadiah, and the date of his cry against Edom is uncertain. A likely date, however, is around 586 BC just after Judah fell to the Babylonians. Then, as at earlier times, the Edomites had treated the people of Judah just as the foreign empires treated her, entering Jerusalem and carrying off her wealth.

The country of Edom was in the dry mountainous region bordering the southern part of the Dead Sea. To most people the land would have been unappealing but the Edomites had learned to survive in their treacherous terrain. They carved elaborate buildings out of the limestone cliffs and conserved water in underground cisterns. Their location gave them a sense of security; their mountains were as forts that could not be penetrated.

Obadiah went to the Edomites, telling them their security was misplaced:

> The pride of your heart has deceived you,
> you who live in the clefts of the rock,
> whose dwelling is high,
> who say in your heart,
> "Who will bring me down to the ground?"
> Though you soar aloft like the eagle,
> though your nest is set among the stars,
> thence I will bring you down, says the Lord
> (Obad. 3-4).

God is sovereign, and he judges people and nations, Obadiah said. "As you have done, it shall be done to you" (Obad. 15). There would be no survivors of the house of Esau, Obadiah predicted, but some would survive from Mount Zion (Jerusalem). Mount Zion would rule over Mount Esau, but "the kingdom shall be the Lord's" (Obad. 21).

Jonah

The Book of Jonah is named for a man who was a prophet during the reign of Jeroboam II of Israel. (See 2 Kings 14:25.) The book is about Jonah, not by him. It does not contain a collection of sermons but is more like a modern short story written for a practical purpose.

The book tells of God asking Jonah to go to Nineveh, of Jonah's attempt to avoid going there, of the Ninevites repenting when Jonah finally did go and announce that the city was going to be destroyed, and of Jonah's anger when Nineveh did not collapse when he said it would. The book shows the feeling almost any Israelite would have had toward Nineveh at the time of Jonah. Nineveh was capital of the Assyrian Empire, and the Assyrians were enemies of the Israelites. The nation was as ominous to Israel as a funnel-shaped cloud; they were frightened by it and would have liked to see it disappear.

The purpose of the book is to show God's great love for all people and to show that those who know of that love are to share it with those who don't. The book was probably widely circulated during the time of Ezra and Nehemiah. It, and the Book of Ruth, prodded the Jews to think of other races and peoples. In trying to preserve their religion, many were separating themselves from others and failing to realize the responsibility of telling the world about God.

In essence, the Book of Jonah summarizes the message of the greatest of the prophets who understood that God's love embraces all mankind. In this it holds the truth of the New Testament.

Micah

The Book of Micah is highly poetic and named for a prophet who lived in Judah at the same time as Isaiah. Whether the two men ever met is uncertain. Micah was younger than Isaiah and was a commoner rather than from the upper class like Isaiah. Too, he was from the small town of Moresheth while Isaiah was from Jerusalem.

The time of Micah and Isaiah was one of prolonged crisis because of the march of the Assyrian army. Samaria fell to the Assyrians in 722 BC, bringing to an end the country of Israel. Judah, too, would have fallen had God not miraculously intervened when the Assyrian army surrounded Jerusalem. (See 2 Kings 18—19.)

The Book of Micah can be conveniently divided into three parts: Micah 1—3; Micah 4—5; and Micah 6—7.

The first section opens with a cry against the two cities of Jerusalem and Samaria. Those cities should have set examples of integrity; instead they had produced epidemics of corruption. Micah said that because of her sins, Samaria was to become "a heap in the open country" (1:6). And because of Jerusalem's sins, that city too was to become "a heap of ruins" (3:12).

The great evil in the cities was what has been described as "the accursed love of possessing." People even lay awake at night scheming how to get more than they needed from people who had less than enough. The leaders set the pattern for evil. Judges accepted bribes, priests taught anything they were hired to teach, prophets predicted what people paid them to say.

The middle section of the book, chapters 4—5, contains messages of comfort. It speaks of two main subjects, a future nation of peace and a future ruler of peace. In the nation of peace people will flow to the house of God to learn his ways. Weapons of war (swords) will be converted into tools (plowshares), and no person will be afraid of another. The ruler of peace will come, like David of old, from Bethlehem. He will be a shepherd, guarding and protecting his people and providing security for them. There will be no confusion in people's minds, no trusting in idols or wealth or military strength. Enemies will disappear, and peace will prevail.

The last section of the book, chapters 6—7, explains true religion: "What does the Lord require of you/but to do justice, and to love kindness,/and to walk humbly with your God?" (Mic. 6:8). People have tried to substitute other factors, but God has made known what is good. It is to walk humbly with him and to show justice and kindness to fellow creatures.

Like Amos, Micah was a champion of the oppressed. His aim was to make people aware of the monstrosity of injustice. To him right and wrong acts could not be thought of as momentary events; they were dimensions of history. And justice was not simply a value; it was a road, an occupation as constantly necessary as breathing.

Nahum

The Book of Nahum is a dramatic poem about the destruction of Nineveh, capital of Assyria. In vivid language it pictures the soldiers of Nineveh in their scarlet uniforms, their shields gleaming like torches, their chariots darting like lightning. Yet they could not halt the destruction. The wealth of the city, the royal family, even the maids, were swept away. When news of the destruction reached distant lands, people clapped their hands. They could not be sorry, for all had repeatedly felt the sting of Assyrian brutality.

Nothing is known about the writer except what is evident from the poem itself. He was a person who recognized that there is a time for legitimate anger. It is right to feel indignation at wrong.

Exactly when the poem was written is uncertain. It may be a prediction of the fall of Nineveh and could have been written shortly before the city fell, or it could have been written shortly after. The city was defeated by the Medes and the Babylonians in 612 BC. Assyria had been a dominant nation for almost two centuries, but by 612 BC new nations were rising, and Assyria was fading. Media, a forerunner of the Medo-Persian Empire, was developing east of Assyria. The Babylonian Empire was developing south of Assyria. The two nations joined together and succeeded in destroying Nineveh. To Nahum, and all who had suffered under the Assyrians, the victory was a just fate for a city of tyrannical imperialists.

The poem is a rebuke of militarism. It is an outraged cry against oppression. It shows that God does not look calmly on violence, that he executes judgment and maintains justice. The theme is God's indignation against evil. He could not and would not ignore the wrongs done by the Assyrians.

Habakkuk

Habakkuk is written by a man who was tormented by the fact that what he saw in life was not consistent with what he thought a God of justice ought to allow. The book is not a collection of speeches made by a prophet but an approach to God by a man who needed some answers.

Habakkuk lived in Judah during the beginning years of the Babylonian Empire. The poem named for him is written in three structural forms, first dialogue, second a "taunt" song, and third, a psalm. The three parts all follow one theme, that though "it seem slow" (2:3), God's holiness and justice will prevail.

The dialogue section is a conversation between God and Habakkuk. Habakkuk was upset over the violence and lawbreaking he saw in his own country. He could not understand why a holy God wouldn't do something to stop it. God replied that he intended to do something. He was going to punish the Jews by sending the Chaldeans against them. (The Babylonians were sometimes called Chaldeans because the southern portion of Babylonia was named Chaldea.)

That answer astonished Habakkuk. The Babylonians were worse than the Jews. They were idol-worshiping aggressors, "guilty men, whose own might is their god" (Hab. 1:11). They stripped the wealth of small countries and arrogantly depended upon their military strength. How could God use a people worse than the Jews to punish the Jews?

Habakkuk withdrew to a tower to think, praying that God would solve his perplexities. As he thought, God led him to see that the Babylonians too would be punished in time: "the arrogant man shall not abide" (Hab. 2:5).

Then follows the "taunt" song—five stanzas each beginning with the word *woe*. The stanzas are taunts addressed to people who wrong others but who suddenly find themselves trapped and suffering for what they had done. The song has a moral: those who are cruel will experience cruelty.

The final section, the psalm, is in praise of God who, as Habakkuk realized in the dialogue section of the poem, is sovereign over all things. He rewards or punishes people according to their actions although his timetable is not our timetable.

Habakkuk discovered that he could experience God's care and receive strength from God without having to see just how the world's problems were going to be solved.

Zephaniah

Zephaniah, a prophet during the reign of King Josiah (640-609 BC) of Judah, was a grandson of King Hezekiah. He was therefore related to King Josiah and likely lived among the upper class citizens of Jerusalem.

Zephaniah's background probably accounts for the fact that unlike many other prophets he did not directly criticise the king, nor did he show any deep concern for the poor. His main interest was syncretism, the blending of religions. People in Jerusalem looked not to one God but to many. There were "those who bow down on the roofs/to the host of the heavens;/those who bow down and swear to the Lord/and yet swear by Milcom" (Zeph. 1:5).

Because of syncretism Zephaniah predicted doom for the people of Jerusalem (Zeph. 1). Because of syncretism he predicted doom for neighboring peoples as well (Zeph. 2) but added that a humble turning to God could save them. Yet not all would suffer disaster (Zeph. 3): "For I will leave in the midst of you/a people humble and lowly./They shall seek refuge in the name of the Lord" (Zeph. 3:12).

Zephaniah probably spoke in the early years of Josiah's reign before the king discovered the Book of Deuteronomy that inspired him to introduce sweeping religious reforms in his country. (See 2 Kings 22—23.) Artists have sometimes pictured Zephaniah as a prophet with a lamp in his hand because he spoke of God searching Jerusalem with lamps. God searched, Zephaniah said, to find those who thought of him as asleep or inactive, who said, "The Lord will not do good, nor will he do ill" (Zeph. 1:12).

The Book of Zephaniah is written in the kind of poetic form used for funeral songs. The major theme is the Day of the Lord.

The Day of the Lord was a concept spoken of early in Israel's history and mentioned by a number of her prophets. Amos had talked about it asking the Israelites why they wanted it to come. They ought to fear it, he said, because of the way they acted. Zephaniah showed it as a day of punishment for Judah and her neighbors. Neither silver nor gold could deliver people from the day, but there was a way to hide from the wrath of it: "Seek the Lord, . . . seek righteousness, seek humility" (Zeph. 2:3).

Zephaniah's description of the Day of the Lord caused the terms *judgment day* and *doomsday* to develop later, yet in his prophecy he was not speaking of a final end-of-the-world day. Rather he was speaking of a clean-house day, a time of changing those who were willing to be changed: "Yea, at that time I will change the speech of the peoples/to a pure speech,/that all of them may call on the name of the Lord/and serve him with one accord" (Zeph. 3:9).

Haggai

In 538 BC Cyrus the Great of Persia marched into Babylon and freed the people who had been captured and brought there by the Babylonians. The Jews were among those given permission to return to their homeland and rebuild their Temple.

Restoring the Temple was at the top of the dreams of the Jews who made their way back to Jerusalem. But the city of Jerusalem was in such rubble that the dream was pushed aside. Raising a roof over their heads and food for their stomachs took priority. Building the Temple was nudged further and further from their list of necessary acts.

Eighteen years passed, then Haggai appeared on the scene. He began preaching. His subject was the completion of the Temple and the purification of worship. He longed to see the beginning of the kingdom of God that earlier prophets had spoken of, and he saw pure worship in the Temple as necessary preparation. God could not send the wonderful age of blessings and prosperity ruled by a king of righteousness until the right preparations were made.

The book named for Haggai contains four messages, each one expressly dated.

The first was on the first day of the sixth month of the second year that Darius was king of Persia. He addressed his words to Zerubbabel, the governor of Jerusalem and to Joshua, the priest. In that message Haggai agreed that times had been hard. The people had planted much but harvested little. They had food and drink, but never enough to satisfy. They had clothes, but not enough to keep warm. They earned money, but it was as though the money was put in a bag with holes.

Haggai suggested there might be a reason for their continued existence at the poverty level. They had been busy building paneled houses for themselves, but God's house lay in ruins. Letting the Temple stay in decay demonstrated that the people's loyalty and commitment to God was also in a state of decay.

Because of Haggai's promptings, Zerubbabel and Joshua began encouraging the people to build the Temple. By the twenty-fourth day of the same month the Spirit of God had so stirred Zerubbabel, Joshua, and the people, that work had begun.

Haggai's next message that is recorded was delivered on the twenty-first day of the next month. The Temple was under construction but some people were upset because it was not the exquisite structure Solomon's Temple had been. Haggai told them to take courage. All gold and silver belongs to God. The new Temple could grow in splendor. It could become greater than the former Temple even as their own prosperity could grow.

The third message was delivered two months later. It asked the people to put two questions to their priests. The first, does touching something holy make a person holy, received a no answer. The second, does touching something unclean make a person unclean, received a yes answer. Haggai used the answers to emphasize the fact that holiness isn't transferable, but uncleanness is contagious.

The fourth message was delivered the same day as the third. It is a message of hope. Because Zerubbabel was governor of Jerusalem and also was a descendant of David, Haggai looked upon him as the one who might begin the new kingdom. (Zerubbabel descended from David through King Jehoichin who had been taken captive by Nebuchadnezzar. See 2 Kings 24:12; 25:27-30.) Nations were being shaken. Wars were overthrowing thrones. God was acting through it all. It was through God that Zerubbabel had been placed in authority in Jerusalem. He was God's choice. In the shifting nations all around them Zerubbabel was like a signet ring, the symbol of rule, and Haggai dared hope that he was evidence that the kingdom of God had begun.

Zechariah

Zechariah was a prophet at approximately the same time as Haggai, and the two spoke on the same subject: restoring the Temple and purifying worship. Both men are mentioned in the Book of Ezra (6:14) as helping inspire the Jews to rebuild the Temple.

The Book of Zechariah is made up of two parts that are so different scholars sometimes speak of them as 1 Zechariah and 2 Zechariah. The first part, chapters 1—8, contains the words of Zechariah. The second part, chapters 9—14, was probably written later by an unknown author or authors. Unity of subject combines the two parts; both follow the theme of the kingdom of God.

The first section is written in apocalyptic form. It contains visions and illustrations similar to those in Daniel. The visions all have symbolic meanings. In one vision Zechariah saw an angel going out to measure Jerusalem for rebuilding. Another angel interrupted, saying Jerusalem was to be rebuilt without walls; its population was to be too large to be confined within walls, and walls were not needed for defense as God would be her defense. In another vision Zechariah saw Joshua the priest standing dressed in filthy rags. The rags were taken away and replaced with rich apparel just as the sins of people—filthy rags—would be taken away and replaced with robes of righteousness. Through these and other visions described in the book, Zechariah illustrated what the kingdom of God would be like, a kingdom made up of righteous people under the protection of God.

Like Haggai, Zechariah saw the building of the Temple and the restoration of worship as preparation for the coming kingdom of God. He was inspired with the hope that the center of the kingdom would be Jerusalem and that the ruler would be from the house of David. Like Haggai, because Zerubbabel was governor of Jerusalem and was from the house of David, Zechariah believed the kingdom was ready to begin.

Although Zechariah wanted the Temple rebuilt and the Temple ritual restored, his attitude toward worship was the same as that of earlier prophets. He did not see ceremony as a substitute for morals. Because the Temple was being rebuilt people came to him with questions about a fast that was customarily held to mourn the destruction of the Temple. They wondered if the fast should still be held. Zechariah pointed out that Jerusalem had not been destroyed because people had failed to observe fasts. God allowed the destruction because people had failed to have concern for each other. God had always given the same basic message to his prophets, and that message still held priority: "Render true judgments, show kindness and mercy each to his brother, do not oppress the widow, the fatherless, the sojourner, or the poor; and let none of you devise evil against his brother in your heart" (Zech. 7:9-10). Fasts, Zechariah said, should be turned into cheerful feasts of joy and gladness. In God's kingdom they will be times of celebration among people who love truth and peace. People of all tongues will come to that kingdom "to seek the Lord of hosts" (Zech. 8:22).

The second section of Zechariah was probably written after Alexander the Great had made Judah a part of the Greek Empire. (See "Connecting Links Between the Testaments" in this book.) In that period Jews could have felt despair when they looked at history. The Greek Empire was another in the long string of nations that had controlled the Jews, each of them deferring their hope that God's kingdom was about to begin. Yet deferment did not lessen their desire for such a kingdom. They were "prisoners of hope" (Zech. 9:12). Delay could dampen their spirits; hope kept them from doubting the future reality of that kingdom.

The writing in chapters 9—11 of Zechariah moves from subject to subject, but the mixed themes are used as background for conveying facts about the coming kingdom. It will be a secure kingdom. Peope will live in harmony with one another. There will be unity. Weapons will be abolished as there will be no need of them. it will be ruled by the King of peace who will provide for and strengthen his people. The king will come, humble, riding an ass (symbol of royalty, not war). He will come in the form of a servant, and he will offer streams of living water which is the source of spiritual life. (The New Testament Gospel writers quoted many statements from this part of Zechariah because they realized the descriptions fitted Christ. They saw that in Christ the longed-for ruler had come, yet the changing of hearts that would produce the needed unity, harmony, and wordwide peace would be slow, for Christ did not conquer with weapons of war.)

The final three chapters of Zechariah are concerned with the final days of nations. They are chapters of faith that there will be a day of judgment, that evil will be punished, and good will be blessed. And on that day "the Lord will become king over all the earth" (Zech. 14:9).

Malachi

Apart from the book itself nothing is known about the writer of Malachi. Even his name is uncertain since the word *Malachi* means "my messenger" and may not be a personal name; yet, for purposes of study, it is accepted as one. The date of the book is also uncertain. From a few clues in the book, however, most scholars think it was likely written some years after Haggai and Zechariah.

One clue is that the Temple was complete. Malachi did not need to plead that it be built as did Haggai and Zechariah. Another clue is that enough time had passed for the newness of the Temple to wear off. People had become lax and unenthusiastic. Another clue is the form of Malachi's speech. Early prophets had attracted attention with the words, "Thus saith the Lord." As time passed people grew less willing to listen to a prophet just because he said he had a message from God. They could be reached easier through argument and reasoning. To meet the need of the age, Malachi used the same device as the Greek philosopher Socrates—questions and answers. (Some call him the Hebrew Socrates; later rabbis adopted the question and answer method of teaching.)

To begin his discussions Malachi made such statements as, "'I have loved you,' says the Lord" (Mal. 1:2); "You have wearied the Lord with your words" (Mal. 3:13). Each statement caused the people to argue with him. They said they hadn't seen any proof that God loved them, they hadn't said anything they should not have.

The people who entered into the discussions were actively religious. They attended Temple services and made religious observances a prominent part of their lives. But for both priests and people the participation was ritualistic. Their hearts were not in it. They thought there was no actual advantage in serving God, and they couldn't see any flaws in themselves. Malachi's purpose was to change their thoughts and draw them to God.

Part of the problem was the low estate into which the priests had fallen. Malachi had a high view of the priesthood. In the covenant God made with them at the time of Moses, they had been given the position of instructors. "True instruction was in his mouth, and no wrong was found on his lips. He walked with me in peace and uprightness, and he turned many from iniquity. For the lips of a priest should guard knowledge, and men should seek instruction from his mouth, for he is the messenger of the Lord of hosts" (Mal 2:6-7).

Rather than carrying out the covenant, the priests of Malachi's day had lost interest. They were bored serving in the Lord's house. "What a weariness this is" (Mal. 1:13), they said. In addition the people showed no respect for the priests. They failed to bring tithes, and the gifts they made were ones they would have been ashamed to offer elsewhere. They vowed their best, yet substituted their worst.

The attitude toward tithes and gifts was symbolic of their general indifference toward God and was reflected in their home life. Marriages were breaking up and the sancity of the home destroyed.

Malachi is the only Old Testment book that condemns divorce. Marriage is described as a covenant of faithfulness between a man and his wife that should be sustained. (In this the writer proclaimed the same attitude that Christ would voice almost 500 years later.) The book also emphasizes several other points that show insights most other prophets did not mention. One is on the fatherhood of God. "Have we not all one father? Has not one God created us? Why then are we faithless to one another?" (Mal. 2:10). Another is that all true worship is offered to God.

Throughout the book, Malachi confronted the problem of people believing that God paid no attention to whether anyone was good or bad. At the beginning he spoke of the Edomites who had been evil, and their evil was repaid with suffering. Later in the book he spoke of the Day of the Lord in which there would be a final judgment. On that day those who have feared God would see justice meted out. They would see that God had kept a record, "a book of remembrance" (Mal. 3:16), and those who had served God would be recorded there. God "will spare them as a man spares his son who serves him" (Mal. 3:17), but on that day the wicked will become like stubble burning in an oven.

Before that day comes God will send a messenger to prepare the way. He will purify, cleanse, refine, so that Judah and Jerusalem will be pleasing to the Lord.

Daily Bible Reading Schedule

Week 24
Hosea 1:1-11
Hosea 4:1-14
Hosea 6:4-6; 7:11-16
Hosea 8:4-7; 10:12-13
Hosea 14:1-9
Joel 1:14-20
Joel 2:12-29

Week 25
Amos 1:1-3,6,9,11,13
Amos 3:1-8; 4:1-9
Amos 5:4-7,14-15
Amos 5:21-24; 6:4-7
Amos 7:7-15; 8:4-6
Obad. 1-14
Obad. 15-21

Week 26
Jonah 1:1-9
Jonah 2—3
Mic. 1:1-9
Mic. 2:1-9
Mic. 3:1-12
Mic. 5:7-15
Mic. 6:6-8

Week 27
Nah. 1:1-11
Nah. 3:1-7
Nah. 3:18-19
Hab. 1:1-11
Hab. 1:12-17
Hab. 2:18 to 3:6
Hab. 3:6-19

Week 28
Zeph. 1:1-9
Zeph. 1:10-18
Zeph. 2:1-7
Zeph. 3:1-7
Zeph. 3:11-18
Hag. 1
Hag. 2

Week 29
Zech. 1:1-21
Zech. 13
Mal. 1
Mal. 2
Mal. 3:1-13
Mal. 3:14-18
Mal. 4

Suggested Topics for Further Research

Behistun Rock: cliff containing carvings that provided key to cuneiform
Canon: officially recognized list of sacred books
Dead Sea Scrolls: oldest copies of Scripture books known to exist
Edom: country founded by Esau
False prophets: prophets who did not speak the word of God
Nineveh: capital of Assyria
Petra: rock city in Edom
Rosetta stone: carved stone that provided key to hieroglyphics
Samaritans: people of the country of Samaria
Septuagint: Greek translation of Scriptures made around 200 BC
Talmud: collection of Jewish writings pertaining to the Scriptures
Zerubbabel's Temple: second Jewish Temple built in Jerusalem

Reinforce Your Memory

Write a line of information about each of the minor prophets:

Hosea

Joel

Amos

Obadiah

Jonah

Micah

Nahum

Habakkuk

Zephaniah

Haggai

Zechariah

Malachi

Draw a map in the space below marking the countries where these prophets preached.

Connecting Links Between the Old and New Testaments

Chart 18.
Between the Old and New Testaments

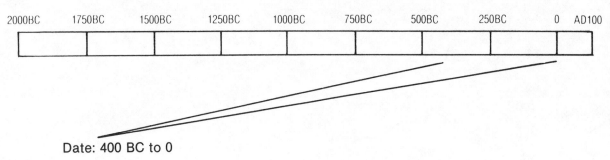

2000BC	1750BC	1500BC	1250BC	1000BC	750BC	500BC	250BC	0 AD100

Date: 400 BC to 0

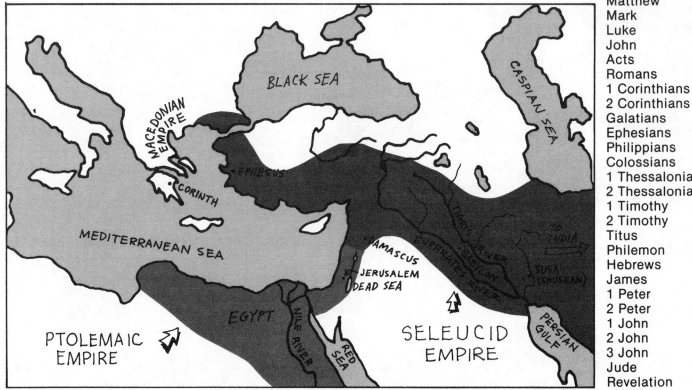

Before turning to the New Testament, the person who wants the Bible to become easy to use needs to look at a number of events that took place between the end of the Old Testament and the beginning of the New. The history recorded in the Old Testament ends with the Persian Empire in power. The New Testament opens approximately 400 years later. Changes that took place during those 400 years cast a major influence over the New Testament. Particularly important were two peninsulas that reach like pointing fingers down into the Mediterranean Sea, Greece and Italy. Although those lands meant almost nothing to the Jews in the days of the Old Testament, they gained great relevance before the time of the New.

The first to cast an influence was Greece. For many years Greece was made up of small independent kingdoms, city-states such as Athens and Sparta. The small kingdoms were eventually joined together into one nation by Philip, king of Macedonia, the northern portion of Greece. (The city of Philippi, to which the New Testament book of Philippians is addressed, was named for him.) He was able to unite the city-states mostly because he was able to convince the people that they should join together to punish Persia because of attacks the Persians had made on the city-states. Philip did not live to carry out his plans of defeating Persia. But he left a son who was one of the superior military geniuses of all time, twenty-year-old Alexander who has come down in history as Alexander the Great.

Within ten years Alexander developed the largest empire the world had seen. It incorporated a vast triangle stretching from Greece down across Egypt in one direction and to the borders of India in the other. (See map, chart 18.) The land of the Jews was, of course, included.

The influence of Alexander over biblical people was massive. His conquest was more than a conquest of territory. It was an infusion of Greek culture, a culture known as Hellenism from Hellas, the name the ancient Greeks called their land.

As a youth Alexander had been taught by Aristotle, the Greek philosopher known as the father of science. Aristotle had been taught by Plato, who had been taught by Socrates. Through the chain of teachers Hellenistic learning had been passed to the young Alexander and he considered it his divine mission to spread that learning. Where he went, Hellenism also went, the language, the ideas, the gymnasiums. (The New Testament was written in Greek because of the spread of Hellenism. The Western world is still affected by Hellenism, architecturally, philosophically, artistically, intellectually, athletically.)

The Greek Empire is the fourth of the great empires that affected the Jews between the time of the Divided Kingdom and the time of Christ.

The March of the Empires

First: Assyria
Second: Babylonia
Third: Persia
Fourth: Greece

Little is known about how Alexander conquered the Jews. There is no historical evidence that the Jews suffered under Alexander's rule. But in 323 BC Alexander died of a fever at the age of thirty-two, and no giant lived who could replace him. The empire was split into four parts, each ruled by one of Alexander's generals. Two of those generals began dynasties that affected the Jews. One was Ptolemy who began ruling Egypt. The other was Seleucus who began ruling Syria.

The Jewish territory, directly between the two, became a battleground between the Ptolemaic and Seleucid kingdoms. Sometimes the Jewish land was ruled by the Ptolemies, other times by the Seleucids. Usually they managed to continue practicing their own religion and to observe their own religious holidays, but that changed when, while the Seleucids ruled them, Antiochus Epiphanes rose to the throne. (There were several Seleucid rulers named Antiochus; cities were called Antioch in their honor.)

Antiochus Epiphanes had dreams of establishing an empire as large as Alexander the Great had ruled. To help unify his kingdom he ordered that everyone under his authority adopt the Greek religion. Statues of Greek gods and goddesses were put in every city and town. In Jerusalem a statue was even placed in the Temple. To the Jews that was an "abomination that makes desolate" (Dan. 11:31).

(The Book of Daniel is closely associated with this period in history. The dream section of the book refers to the Greeks, to the division of the empire into four parts, and to the ruler who desecrated the holy places. Daniel was quite likely written during this time and became an important source of encouragement for the Jews facing the difficulties of the age.)

Under Antiochus Epiphanes the Jews were not allowed to practice any of their religious customs such as circumcising their infant sons. They could not observe their religious holidays, not even the sabbath. And anyone caught with a copy of the Scriptures was sentenced to die. Many Jews chose death rather than obey the orders. An age of agony began.

The age of agony began to come to an end when a Seleucid officer ordered Mattathias, an old Jewish priest, to sacrifice a pig to a statue. Mattathias refused. Another Jew stepped forward to perform the rite. In a sudden burst of anger old Mattathias rushed upon the Jew, killed him, and also killed the Seleucid officer. He then fled to the hills followed by his five sons. They were soon joined by hundreds of Jews who wanted to fight for religious freedom. Using guerilla warfare, they began winning battle after battle and gradually succeeded in freeing their land. (The Seleucids were having difficulties in several areas and could not totally concentrate on the Jews; nevertheless, much of the success was due to Jewish bravery and determination.)

The Jews began a period of self-rule, the first since the time of the kings told about in the Old Testament Books of Kings. The sons of old Mattathias, one after the other, became the rulers. They were called Maccabees, a nickname that probably means hammer, although their real name was Hasmonean. Under the Maccabees the country grew until it became almost as large as the United Kingdom had been under King Solomon. The kingdom lasted a hundred years, from 164 to 63 BC.

(The account of the Jewish revolt under the Maccabees is given in 1 Maccabees, a book of the Apocrypha.)

The Maccabean victory caused a new holiday to be added to the yearly festivals of the Jews. It is the only religious holiday not mentioned in the Bible. Called Hanukkah, or the Feast of Lights, the festival commemorates the day Jerusalem was freed from Seleucid rule and the Temple cleansed so it could once more be used in the worship of God.

Tradition says that when the Temple was cleansed only one small container of oil could be found. It held enough fuel to keep the Temple lamp burning for one day, but it miraculously burned for eight days. For that reason Hanukkah is celebrated for eight days each year. Eight candles are lighted, one additional each evening, until all eight are burning on the last evening.

Hanukkah comes near the Christian celebration of Christmas, a fact that has caused the festival to increase in popularity in recent years. It has become a time of gift giving for Jews just as Christmas has become a time of gift giving for Christians.

While the Maccabean Kingdom was flourishing, the peninsula of Italy was rapidly becoming prominent. Its chief city was Rome, and the country that had developed was called the Roman Republic. Around 100 BC, Julius Caesar, perhaps the greatest Roman who ever lived, was born. When he became an adult, he became famous among the Romans as a speaker and writer (his "Works on the Gallic Wars" are still required reading for most Latin students), two tasks he enjoyed. But he knew that to really become famous and to become a leader in the Roman Republic, he would have to fight for his country. He led armies northward through central Europe and into England, claiming the entire territory for Rome.

At the same time another Roman general, Pompey, was taking other lands for Rome. He conquered Spain, parts of Greece, Turkey, and the Seleucid Kingdom.

The Jews watched the progress of Rome with approval. They thought of the Romans as friends, not as a threat. But Rome did not have the same benign attitude toward the Jews. Pompey sent an army to Jerusalem and soon took the Maccabean Kingdom for Rome. Rome is the fifth of the major nations that affected the Jews between the time of the Divided Kingdom and the time of Christ. Rome began ruling the Jews in 63 BC.

> The March of the Empires
> First: Assyria
> Second: Babylonia
> Third: Persia
> Fourth: Greece
> Fifth: Rome

After the Romans conquered the Maccabean Kingdom, Julius Caesar appointed a king to rule over the Jews. The king he chose was Antipater, an Idumaean (Greek for Edomite). The choice was distasteful to Jews. Idumaeans and Jews had been enemies for generations. The hatred could be traced back to ancient feuds between Jacob, from whom the Jews descended, and his twin brother, Esau, from whom the Idumaeans descended. (See Gen. 27.) Tension between the two peoples had increased through the years because the Idumaeans repeatedly mistreated the Jews. (See Num. 20:14-21 and Obad. 9-14.)

Neither Julius Caesar nor Antipater ruled long. Both were assassinated. In the turmoil that followed Caesar's death, two men who had been close to Caesar emerged as leaders. One was Antony, Caesar's friend who is best known today because of his romantic link with Cleopatra, Egypt's queen. (Cleopatra was the last of the Ptolemy rulers.) The other was Octavian, the nephew and adopted son of Julius Caesar.

The two ruled together for a short time with Antony in charge of the southern area which included the land of the Jews and Octavian in charge of the northern area. Antony appointed a new king to rule the Jews, Herod, the son of Antipater, a choice that again displeased the Jews.

Antony and Octavian might have continued ruling jointly for some time had Octavian not gotten angry with Antony because of his involvement with Cleopatra. Octavian declared war on Antony, and defeated Antony's navy in a sea battle. Antony and Cleopatra both committed suicide, and Octavian became sole ruler of the Roman Republic. Herod expressed his loyalty to Octavian and was allowed to continue ruling the Jews.

Octavian is better known today as Caesar Augustus. He took the name Caesar because of his relationship to Julius Caesar. His people honored him by calling him Augustus, a title of respect usually reserved for Roman gods.

Under Caesar Augustus the Roman Republic became the Roman Empire. Augustus gave it the new title because he said the nation had become too large and powerful to be thought of as anything less than an empire. (See chart 19.) The date was 27 BC.

The New Testament opens with Caesar Augustus in charge of the empire and with Herod, who became known as Herod the Great, in charge of the land of the Jews. Hellenistic influence had made Greek the dominant language in the entire vicinity of the Mediterranean Sea. Rome had united the same area under one central government. For the Jews the time was one of unrest. They had enjoyed self-rule under the Maccabees. And they looked back upon their history of long years before when they had been ruled by their ideal king, David. They longed for a messiah, a new David, who would free them from foreign dominion.

Reinforce Your Memory

Between the Old and New Testaments two major empires arose that affected the Jews of the Bible. The first was the _____ ruled by _____ the _____. It divided into four parts after a short time and two of the parts affected the Jews, the area ruled by _____ and the area ruled by _____.

Antiochus Epiphanes, ruler of the _____, caused the Jews great misery. They fought against him, won, and began the _____ Kingdom. A new holiday was begun: _____.

The next nation to affect the Jews was the _____. The ruler who first called the nation an empire was _____ _____. Under him _____ the Great served as king of the Jews.

Draw a timeline indicating the approximate date of the Greek rule over the Jews and the beginning of Roman rule over them.

Draw a map showing the Greek Empire and the two kingdoms that influenced the Jews after the Greek Empire divided into parts.

SECTION 5

The First Five Books of the New Testament

The Old Testament centers around a particular group of people, the Jews. The New Testament focuses upon one person born among the descendants of the Jews, Jesus Christ. The first five books of the New Testament contain four accounts of the life of Jesus and one account of the thirty years following his ascension.

The first four books in the New Testament, commonly called Gospels, each give a separate account of the life of Jesus. The word *gospel* originally meant a gift to a person who brought good news. Later the word began to stand for the good news itself, but after Jesus was born *gospel* became a synonym for a biography of Jesus.

The first three of the four Gospels, Matthew, Mark, and Luke, are so similar they are often called the *Synoptic* Gospels meaning "see alike." In general, the three Synoptics record the same basic information in similar order and using similar words. Mark, however, is shorter than the other two, and many scholars believe it was written first. One reason is that Matthew and Luke together contain all but about thirty verses of Mark which makes it seem they chose to follow Mark's presentation but to add more information.

An important difference in the three Synoptics is that each was written for different readers. Matthew is directed toward Jews, Mark toward persons who want a rapid overview of Christ's life, and Luke toward non-Jews.

The Fourth Gospel, John, is unlike the Synoptics. Eusebius, a fourth-century bishop who wrote the world's first history of Christianity gave a possible reason. He said that Matthew, Mark, and Luke were written first. John read those Gospels and, since he was familiar with facts they had not mentioned, recorded those facts.

Jesus lived approximately thirty-three years. Two of the Gospels, Matthew and Luke, mention facts about Jesus' birth; and one of them, Luke, mentions an event in his childhood, but mainly all four Gospels concentrate on the last years of Jesus' life. In those years he taught, preached, and healed throughout the territory that had, centuries before, been known as Canaan. All four Gospels conclude with Jesus' last visit to Jerusalem where jealous religious leaders conspired against him and put him to death, but on the third day he rose from the dead.

The aim of the Gospels is to set forth the message of salvation through Jesus Christ. The writers used historical and biographical information for this purpose. They were not attempting to preserve a record of the past, but to help readers meet the Savior. They tell of the mighty works that Jesus did, and in so doing they show that Jesus is the Son of God who was infused with God's power and used it to help people when he was on earth. Jesus' teachings are presented, not as a record of exactly what he said on a given day, but to show the way of life he came to give to all who would accept it. His personality makes its own appeal to the heart and understanding.

The fifth book in the New Testament, Acts, begins where the Gospels end. It tells what happened next.

Acts is actually a continuation of Luke; it was written by the same author. But because all four Gospels tell about Christ and only one book tells what happened in the years that followed, Acts is essentially a continuation of each of the Gospels. Each Gospel gives the good news of Jesus Christ which resulted in the formation of the Christian church. Acts gives the history of the church being formed. Without

116

Acts we would know little of the initial organization of the church, the opposition it met, the meeting of its early leaders to work on problems that arose, the first missionaries and where they traveled. Acts makes the rest of the New Testament clearer because it provides the background for the books that come after it. It is the connecting link between the Gospels and the remaining books of the New Testament. The book covers approximately the same length of time as the Gospels, ending around AD 65.

In studying the Gospels and Acts it is a help to become acquainted with the names of rulers of the countries that are important in the books and with the locations of the countries. It is also helpful to become familiar with the principle religious viewpoints of the Jews who were living at the time.

The main area of activity throughout the New Testament was, of course, the Roman Empire. During the time covered in the Gospels and Acts five different men held the title of Emperor of Rome: Caesar Augustus, Tiberius, Caligula, Claudius, and Nero. The men who held ruling offices under the emperors went by a number of titles. Of those who ruled the Jews some were called kings, other tetrarchs (rulers of a part, usually one fourth), and others procurators (governor).

Herod the Great, who ruled the entire Jewish area when Jesus was born, went by the title king. He is mentioned very few times in the Gospels, yet he became the best known of all the Herods. (Seven Herods ruled during the New Testament period, all related.) His name became known for two very opposite acts: one was destructive; the other, constructive. First, after Jesus was born, he sent soldiers to Bethlehem with orders to kill all male children under two years of age. The act was not strange for Herod; he had killed some of his best friends, his wife Mariamne, and even two of his own sons. Yet because it was Jesus that he tried to kill in the Bethlehem slaughter, Herod's name became known. The second reason Herod's name became known is because he remodeled the Temple at Jerusalem, making it into one of the world's most beautiful buildings. He named it for himself.

Josephus, a Jewish historian who lived in Jerusalem when the Temple was new, described it in great detail. He said the site was originally a steep rocky incline but that a wall of massive stones had been built and the area filled in to make a broad level plain. The highest elevation to the lowest was so great, said Josephus, that if any looked down from "those altitudes, he would be giddy, while his sight could not reach to such an immense depth." The entire level plain was enclosed with towering walls. Inside there were wide open courtyards and long, covered colonnades. The columns were made of white marble and were "of the Corinthian order, and caused amazement, by reason of the grandeur." The main gate way was covered with gold. It was a hundred feet high and forty feet wide, and it had no doors, "for it represented the universal visibility of heaven." The wall was also covered with gold, and golden vines clung to it "from which clusters of grapes hung as tall as a man's height." The Temple building, said Josephus, "appeared to strangers, when they were coming to it at a distance, like a mountain covered with snow; for as to those parts of it that were not gilt, they were exceeding white." Anyone was allowed in the main courtyard, only Jews in an inner yard, only male Jews in Temple proper, and only priests in the inner chamber. In the building were embroidered curtains "of a context that was truly wonderful." The colors and materials represented the universe. Scarlet represented fire, flax the earth, blue the air, purple the sea.

Herod also built Caesarea (named for Caesar Augustus), a seaport on the Mediterranean coast. In that area of the world, silt washes toward the shore creating hazardous conditions for ships. To overcome the difficulty Herod had a curved stone wall projected out into the water and developed an artificial bay. The protected harbor that resulted became the Roman capital of the area.

After Herod the Great died, the land he had ruled was divided into three sections. Three of Herod's sons became tetrarchs, each having charge of one of the areas. The particular lands in these three sections are very important to the Gospels because it was in those areas that Jesus traveled during his years of teaching, preaching, and healing. (See chart 20.)

One section was ruled by Herod Philip who is mentioned only once in the Gospels (Luke 3:1). He was probably the best of Herod's sons, and he ruled the northeastern portion of the land his father had ruled. Jesus traveled in that area and an important city, Caesarea Philippi (named for Caesar Augustus and Herod Philip), was there at the foot of the highest elevation in the country, Mount Hermon.

Another section consisted of three small areas, Judea (Greek for Judah), Samaria (named for the former capital of Israel), and Idumaea (Greek for Edom). It was ruled by Herod Archelaus, but he proved to be a temperamental tyrant like his father, so Rome replaced him with a procurator. Several procurators who used Caesarea as their capital served during the lifetime of Jesus, but the only one important to the Gospels was Pontius Pilate who sentenced Jesus to death. He was one of the most effective procurators who ruled the Jews, yet he was too weak to stand up against the Jews who wanted Jesus dead even though "he knew that it was out of envy that they had delivered him up" (Matt. 27:18).

The remaining section was ruled by Herod Antipas. He is mentioned in the Gospels more than any of the other Herods, mostly because of his cruelty. (See Matt. 14:1-12; Luke 9:7; 23:7-15.) Under his authority were Galilee and Perea. Galilee is especially important in the New Testament because Jesus grew up there and did a great deal of his work there. Perea was the area most Jews traveled through when they went from Galilee to Jerusalem for religious festivals. They would not take the more direct route through Samaria because of the ancient animosity between the Jews and the Samaritans.

Prejudices of varying kinds existed during the time of Jesus. In addition to the attitude of the Jews and Samaritans toward each other, there was the hatred Jews felt toward the Romans because the Romans ruled over them. Some Jews were known as Zealots because they had "zeal" for Jewish freedom from Roman rule. Besides attitudes of this kind there were religious prejudices among Jews with differing viewpoints. Particularly important were the views of two groups, the Sadducees and the Pharisees.

The two views went far back in history just as did the beginning of the Samaritan and Jewish hatred. No information is available that tells just how the two views started or how the groups acquired the names they were known by although they probably began as early as the time of Ezra and Nehemiah. Both groups were definitely in existence by the time of the Greek rule. The primary differences in the two were related to, first of all, the Scriptures, and second, to Greek influence.

The Sadducees were narrow in their view of the Scriptures and broad in their view of Greek culture. They said the Scriptures should be limited to the books of Moses: Genesis, Exodus, Leviticus, Numbers, and Deuteronomy. They called those books the Torah, a word meaning teaching. (Jews still call the first five books of the Bible the Torah.) They recognized no other religious writings; they were completely closed to all others. They were open, however, to new ideas brought in by the Greeks. The Greeks introduced plays and gymnasiums to the Jews. The Sadducees accepted both and were pleased with them. They enrolled their children in gymnastic classes and spent evenings at the theater.

The Pharisees, on the other hand, were horrified at the thought of naked wrestling matches in the gyms and the acting of imaginary stories on stage. They were certain such things could do nothing but pervert the minds of youth. Toward Scripture, however, their outlook was broad. They accepted not only the Torah, but Joshua, Judges, Kings and the writings of certain poets and prophets. In addition, they added the Oral Law, a group of laws developed to help them know how to obey the Torah. The Oral Law, and the acceptance of other books besides the Torah, gave the Pharisees a religious flexibility that was not found among the Sadducees.

In addition to holding different views, the two groups also held different economic levels. The Sadducees were quite wealthy, the Pharisees were from the middle class. Neither group approved of Jesus. Generally they were too busy standing up for their traditions to hear what he had to say or to look with an open mind at what he did.

Another group of people frequently mentioned in the Gospels and Acts are scribes. A scribe was once a kind of sidewalk letter writer who was paid to write documents or to copy them. By the time of Jesus the main work of scribes was to copy the Scripture and to teach it. They had become religious leaders even though they were not of the priesthood.

The Jewish court known as the Sanhedrin was important at the time of Christ. It was a religious court made up of seventy men with the high priest serving as executive director. It met in an impressive room in the colonnade section of the Temple. It primarily decided on problems that arose in connection with religious law. It had tremendous power and could even sentence a person to death although that sentence had to have Roman approval before it could be carried out.

One of the principle people told about in the Gospels is John the Baptist whose preaching prepared the way for the coming of Christ. Others important in the Gospels are the twelve men called apostles who spent a great deal of time with Jesus learning from him and about him. Not a great deal is told about any of them, although Peter was the undisputed leader of the group.

The Gospels and Acts are the climatic books of the entire Bible. Everything else leads up to the coming of Christ and to the kingdom of God his coming ushered in.

Daily Bible Reading Schedule

Week 30
Matt. 1:1-25
Matt. 2
Matt. 3
Matt. 4
Matt. 5
Matt. 6:1-15
Matt. 7:1-12

Week 31
Matt. 8:1-17
Matt. 9:9-26
Matt. 12:22-37
Matt. 13:18-23,36-43
Matt. 15:1-20
Matt. 17:1-13
Matt. 18:1-14

Week 32
Mark 7:1-22
Mark 10:1-16
Mark 11:1-11
Mark 13:1-10
Luke 1:1-25
Luke 1:26-56
Luke 1:57-80

Week 33
Luke 2:1-21
Luke 2:22-40
Luke 9:18-26
Luke 10:25-37
Luke 15:1-10
Luke 15:11-20
Luke 20:1-26

Week 34
Luke 22:1-13
Luke 22:14-37
Luke 22:39-62
Luke 23:1-12
Luke 23:26-49
Luke 23:50 to 24:11
Luke 24:13-52

Week 35
John 1:1-18
John 3:1-21
John 8:1-40
John 11:1-52
John 19
John 20
John 21

Suggested Topics for Further Research

Alexander the Great: king of the Greek Empire
Ptolemaic Kingdom: one of the countries carved from Alexander's nation
Seleucid Kingdom: another country carved from Alexander's nation
Antiochus Epiphanes: ruler of the Seleucids who persecuted Jews
Maccabean Kingdom: Jewish country between 164-63 BC
Julius Caesar: ruler of the Roman Republic
Pompey: general who claimed the Jewish land for Rome
Marc Antony: friend of Julius Caesar, coruler with Octavian
Octavian: nephew of Julius Caesar who became the Augustus Caesar of the Bible,
    first ruler of the Roman Empire
Pharisees: Jews of a particular religious view
Sadducees: Jews of a particular religious view
Essenes: Jews of a particular religious view
Zealots: Jews with "zeal" for political freedom

Chart 19.
Matthew, Mark, Luke, John, Acts

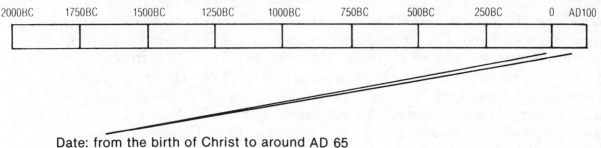

Date: from the birth of Christ to around AD 65

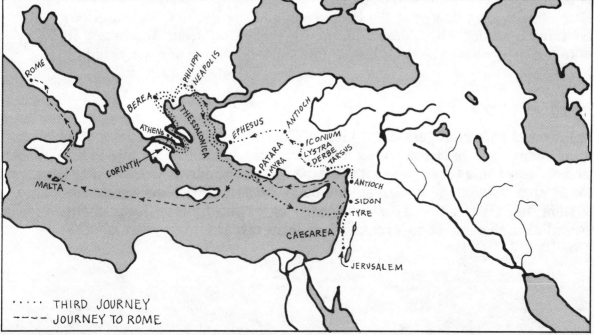

- - - - FIRST JOURNEY
· · · · · SECOND JOURNEY

Paul's First and Second Journeys

· · · · · THIRD JOURNEY
- - - - JOURNEY TO ROME

Paul's Third Journey and His Journey to Rome

Matthew

Matthew, the first of the four books in the New Testament containing brief accounts of the life of Jesus, was originally written specifically for Christians who had a Jewish background. The writer quoted often from the Old Testament which was a natural thing to do for Jews. (Compare Matt. 1:23 with Isa. 7:14; Matt. 2:6 with Micah 5:2; Matt. 3:3 with Isa. 40:3.) Much attention in the book is given to the fact that Jesus fulfilled the Old Testament prophecies concerning the Messiah. A frequently recurring statement says, "All this took place to fulfil what the Lord had spoken by the prophet" (1:22; 2:15; 26:56). Such references helped Jewish converts to understand that faith in Christ did not require the rejection of the Old Testament but was the goal toward which the Old Testament pointed.

Attention is also given to building up the church. Matthew is the only Gospel that speaks of the church directly (16:18; 18:17).

The book was put together with great artistry and care. Its style is smooth and quotable and lends itself to teaching. It follows the chronological order of Jesus' life (in this it is almost identical to Mark) but groups the teachings of Jesus according to topics. Matthew wanted to convey facts about Jesus' life, but he was more interested in presenting his teachings. Because of the detailed teachings given in Matthew the book is as much a manual on the Christian faith as an account of Jesus' life.

Matthew opens with the kind of beginning once common in many Jewish books—a long list of names. Such lists were important to Jews. On them they based claims to kingship, priesthood, and property rights. More importantly the lists had theological significance showing God's continuous relationship with his people and the fulfilling of his promises. Matthew's list shows the main divisions of Jewish history, from Abraham to David, from David to the Babylonian War, and from the Babylonian War to the birth of Christ. By giving the list Matthew provided both the religious and the historical background for his book. By reading the list, Jews knew the time setting of the book and that the subject was associated with their own people and their God.

The main body of the book can be divided into five sections. (Perhaps Matthew followed the five group patterns of the Pentateuch and the Book of Psalms.) Each group contains a section about Jesus' life and a section on Jesus' teachings. In addition to the five groups, the book has an introductory section and a concluding section.

Introduction: Matthew 1—2

The introductory section tells of the birth of Christ in Bethlehem, of Wise Men visiting the young child, of Herod killing infants in Bethlehem in an attempt to kill Jesus, and of Jesus being taken to Egypt to escape Herod's slaughter. Matthew is the only Gospel that tells of these events. (Although modern Christmas scenes frequently show the visit of the Wise Men occurring at the time of Jesus' birth, Matthew indicates they may have arrived when Jesus was about two years of age.)

Part 1: Matthew 3—7

The main body of the book begins with Jesus' baptism, temptation, and the calling of his first disciples. The teaching included in this section has come to be called the "Sermon on the Mount" (chapters 5—7). The sermon deals with how people ought to live and includes some of the most-often quoted portions of all New Testament Scripture: the Beatitudes (5:3-12), the Lord's Prayer (6:9-14), the Golden Rule (7:12).

Part 2: Matthew 8—12

Following the Sermon on the Mount, Matthew again took up the biography of Jesus and told of his travels in Galilee where he healed people in one town after another. Jesus then took his disciples aside and instructed them and sent them out to teach.

Part 3: Matthew 11—13

The next biography section contains information about Jesus answering questions put to him by John's disciples and also belligerent questions from Pharisees who continually tried to discredit and confuse him. The biography portion is followed by a series of parables (stories to illustrate points) that Jesus told to help people learn about God. Often those who heard the parables did not grasp the meaning; even the disciples asked Jesus to explain some of them. But the stories were easy to remember, and by thinking about them people could gain understanding at later times. The topics of the parables were never distant and abstract but were on subjects familiar to the listeners—planting seeds, gathering crops, making bread, fishing. Most of the parables were used to teach about the kingdom of heaven—the kingdom made up of people who obey God, who have acquired natures like God's nature, who treat each other with compassion and kindness.

Part 4: Matthew 14—18

The fourth biographical section tells of some of the most moving moments in Jesus' life—of his pain over the death of John the Baptist, of his attempt to lead his disciples to understand what he meant by "beware of the leaven of the Pharisees and Sadducees" (Matt. 16:5), of his talking with his disciples about his coming death. It is followed by another group of parables which, like the earlier ones, teach about the kingdom of heaven through familiar topics—children, sheep, debts.

Part 5: Matthew 19—25

Section five tells of Jesus leaving Galilee and going to Judea where he taught large crowds and where Pharisees tried to trick him with controversial questions. This section also contains parables on the kingdom of heaven, using such topics as salaries for work, owning property, and a wedding guest list as illustrations. In addition the section contains a series of teachings on the end of the world, a subject that greatly concerned Jesus' disciples. Jesus told them of signs to look for, and lessons to learn from events, but he also assured them "of that day and hour no one knows" (Matt. 24:36).

Conclusion: Matthew 26—28

The concluding section tells of Jesus eating the Passover meal with his disciples in Jerusalem, and of the rapid events that followed—the arrest, trial, crucifixion, death, and resurrection of Christ. The book ends with the words that have come to be known as "the Great Commission," the command Jesus made for all who knew what God had done to go out and teach throughout the world.

Mark

Mark is the briefest and simplest of the four Gospels and contains very little that is not recorded in either Matthew or Luke. Because of that readers have sometimes neglected Mark and have studied the larger volumes of Matthew and Luke, but the compactness of Mark makes it ideal for grasping an overall picture of Christ.

The book is a straightforward account of the life of Jesus. It moves along rapidly as if the writer were bubbling over and too eager to be slowed. It is told almost as a child would tell of events so exciting that words tumble one after another in breathless wonder. There are few pauses. Statement follows statement connected by the word *and*.

Mark includes vivid details that make the account clear and alive. He mentioned that Jesus was sleeping "on a pillow" (Mark 4:38, KJV) when the disciples woke him because of a storm. He spoke of children coming to Jesus and Jesus "took them in his arms" (Mark 10:16). In the description of Jesus feeding the five thousand, Mark mentioned that the people "sat down in groups, by hundreds and by fifties" (Mark 6:40). The other Gospel writers did not mention such minor, but descriptive, points.

Mark's aim was to give a picture of Jesus as he was. The original readers of the Gospel were probably already Christians who wanted a written record of information they had heard only by mouth. The book may have been directed particularly to Roman Christians because the writing contains explanations of Jewish customs that Romans would have needed to have explained to them. (See, for example, Mark 7:3-4 which explains that the Pharisees performed ritualistic washing before eating and conducted a purification ceremony over eating utensils.)

The book begins with the baptism and temptation of Jesus, moves to the period of his ministry in Galilee, and finishes with his going to Jerusalem where he was tried, crucified and buried, then rose from the dead. The word *immediately* occurs about forty times in the book, making the record one of almost continuous action. The writing contains more information about what Jesus did than what he said. The ministry of Jesus, as told by Mark, is similar in form to sermons preached by the early disciples (see Acts 10:34-43). They told of significant events from Jesus' life to prove that he was the Christ. By listening to the accounts of his mighty works those who had ears to hear could understand that God's power was in Jesus, and he was indeed God's instrument for the saving of people from sin.

Luke

Although Luke is classed as a Synoptic Gospel because it is so kin to Matthew and Mark, it has one characteristic that neither of them has in any way. That characteristic is that the book was written as the first part of a two-volume work. The second volume, the Book of Acts, is so related to the Gospel of Luke that any study of one of the books should take into consideration the other. The purpose of each is more evident in the total work than in either alone.

Luke's purpose was to present the entire record of Christianity from its beginning up to the time of his writing. In the first volume he told of the rise of Christianity. In the second volume he told of the spread of Christianity. He opened his writing by explaining why and how he had written. He felt it would be good if he could produce an orderly account of accurate information. He was equipped to do that because for some time he had carefully followed events pertaining to Christianity. In addition he had available books that had been written about it and had heard eyewitnesses talk.

Luke addressed his books to Theophilus who was probably a Roman official who had become a Christian. No doubt Luke also considered the wider world and hoped to appeal to the minds and hearts of people everywhere. The books were obviously written for Gentiles, not Jews. The references to Jewish customs are ones that non-Jews could easily understand, and the Old Testament is hardly quoted at all. Special terms are written in the Greek rather than the Hebrew form so non-Jews could grasp the meaning with ease, for example the Greek word *master* was used rather than the Hebrew word with the same meaning, *rabbi*.

The two volumes were originally separated probably because each filled one scroll. When the New Testament was compiled, the Gospel volume was placed with the other three Gospels, and Acts was placed after them all because it records events that took place later.

The information in Luke is arranged in sections, or blocks. Some of the blocks are almost identical to Mark. Other blocks are on the teachings of Jesus similar to the ones given in Matthew. And still others are sections that are in Luke alone. A brief outline of Luke is as follows:

Luke 1	Why the book was written, prediction and birth of John, the forerunner of Jesus
Luke 2—3	Birth and childhood of Jesus; his baptism and a list of his ancestry
Luke 4—18	The main section beginning with Christ's temptation and continuing through the time that he spent traveling about teaching, preaching, and healing
Luke 19—24	Trip to Jerusalem which culminated in Christ's death and resurrection

Luke has been called the Gospel of Praise because of the radiant hymns included in it. (See quote from Mary, 1:46-55; from Zechariah, 1:68-79; from Simeon, 2:29-32.) It has been called the Gospel of Women because of the way Luke spoke of Elizabeth, Anna, Mary and Martha, and other women. It has been called the Gospel of Prayer because it shows Jesus so often at prayer (Luke 3:2; 5:16; 9:29; 22:32). But most of all it has been called the Gospel of the Whole World because of the way it breaks down barriers and touches people in all walks of life from the rich Zacchaeus to the penitent thief on the cross.

The book presents the character of Christ and his purpose on earth. The teaching of the book is that all people need to be lifted out of their sins and brought back to life and hope. That is what God has offered through Christ.

About half the Gospel of Luke contains information that is not found in any of the other Gospels. It is the most complete volume on the life of Jesus that we possess.

All the Gospel writers spoke of John, the forerunner of Christ whose sermons created a receptive atmosphere for Jesus and who baptized him. But Luke is the only writer who told about John's birth and of his parents. Luke is also the only writer who told of Jesus' birth in a stable, the account that has come to be accepted as "the Christmas story."

Luke contains numerous parables not told about in the other Gospels. Two of the best known are the story of the good Samaritan (Luke 10:30-37) and the story of the prodigal son (Luke 15:11-32).

Among other incidents in Luke that the other Gospel writers did not tell about is an event that occurred at the time of the trial of Jesus. The Roman governor, Pilate, learned that Jesus came from Galilee. Since Pilate did not rule Galilee, he tried to shift the responsibility of what should be done with Jesus to Herod Antipas who ruled both Perea and Galilee at the time. Herod was in Jerusalem so Pilate sent Jesus to him. Herod was glad; for some time he had been wanting to see Jesus perform a miracle. But when Jesus did not put on a show, "Herod with his soldiers treated him with contempt and mocked him; then, arraying him in gorgeous apparel, he sent him back to Pilate. And Herod and Pilate became friends with each other that very day, for before this they had been at enmity with each other" (Luke 23:11-12).

John

The Gospel of John is the last of the four New Testament books that tell of the life of Christ. It is the different Gospel. It has been said that John "is at once the easiest and the hardest book in the Bible to understand." Through the centuries it has had meaning for humble peasants and at the same time messages for the most advanced theologians.

The book is different in content from the other Gospels. It omits much that they tell about. It does not mention the birth, baptism, or temptation of Jesus. It does not mention preparing for the Last Supper. And it contains no parables at all.

126

On the other hand John included much that the other Gospel writers did not. The other writers told mostly of time Jesus spent in Galilee. John told mostly of time Jesus spent in Judea, particularly in Jerusalem. The other Gospels mentioned only one Passover celebration: John mentioned three (2:13; 6:4; 11:52), showing that the ministry of Jesus covered a longer period of time than seems apparent from the Synoptics. The other three Gospel writers named the disciples but told little about them. John did not list their names but told some things they did and said. He also mentioned other people the Synoptics did not, Nicodemus (chapter 3), for instance, and the woman of Samaria (chapter 4). Too, John is the only Gospel writer who told of the raising of Lazarus from the dead.

The form of the book is different from the other Gospels. In the Synoptics the biography of Jesus is prominent. In John it is not the biography but the meaning of Christ's life that is emphasized. The Synoptics stress the humanity of Jesus, John the divinity. John stated that the world itself couldn't hold all the books that would be written if all that Christ did were told. Yet he had no desire to write about all that Christ did. He wanted only to tell enough to lead people to know that Jesus Christ is the Son of God and that through belief in him people can become children of God, "born, not of blood nor of the will of the flesh nor of the will of man, but of God" (John 1:12). He therefore chose to tell a few incidents and used them as illustrations of everlasting truths.

John began his presentation, not with Jesus' birth or with the first moments of his ministry but with God before the world was made. He linked Christ with God through all time calling him the Word of God, a term of magnificent proportions standing for the mind, or thought, of God. "No one has ever seen God" (John 1:18), but he is perfectly reflected in the Word. As the Word, Christ is the embodiment of God's mind and thought, the totality of who God is, the producer of life and light, the wholeness of grace and truth. Christ came that people might know God and that individuals might experience the fullness that life is meant to be.

Throughout the Gospel John spoke of "signs" Jesus performed that showed who he is. He turned water into wine, "the first of his signs" (John 2:11). He healed, and "a multitude followed him, because they saw the signs which he did on those who were diseased" (John 6:2). The chief priests and the Pharisees were afraid everyone would believe in him because he performed "many signs" (John 11:47).

Each time John presented a sign, he followed it with a long discussion. Sometimes the discussions enlarged upon the meaning of the signs. Sometimes they involved questions and arguments presented by people who were hostile toward Christ. Sometimes they involved questions Jesus put to others in order to teach them.

John arranged the material in the book in the way that he did to show that the signs were not just momentary events but were illustrations of eternal truths. Jesus healed a blind man and although that was a historical event at a particular time, Jesus has continued to offer light to all people because he is the light of the world.

Jesus fed 5000 people in one day, yet every day he offers unperishable food to all people because he is the Bread of life. He raised Lazarus from the dead, and in addition he offers eternal life to all people because he is the resurrection and the life.

The book can be summarized in the best-known verse that it contains, "For God so loved the world that he gave his only Son, that whoever believes in him should not perish but have eternal life" (John 3:16). God sent Christ because he wants people to be rescued from their sins, not condemned because of them. The aim of the Gospel of John is to help people enter into the personal relationship with Christ that will transform their very existence.

Acts

The Book of Acts is the second half of the two-volume work written by Luke, the first half being the Gospel of Luke. Like the Gospel, Acts is directed to Theophilus, a person whose identity we do not now know but who probably was an important and influential Gentile.

Acts is not a sequel to Luke in the sense that years after writing his Gospel, Luke decided to tell about later events. Instead the Book of Acts directly follows the Gospel of Luke. Probably the two books were planned and written near the same time. Together Luke-Acts comprises more than one fourth of the New Testament making Luke the author of more New Testament writings than any other one person.

Luke gathered the material for Acts in the same way he did for the Gospel of Luke. He had personal interviews with various people and read all material he could find on the subject. In addition, in writing Acts, he was able to add firsthand information. He himself was present during several of the occasions that he wrote about. (Those occasions are evident from his use of the pronoun "we." See Acts 21 and Acts 27.)

The name Acts, or as the book is often called, the "Acts of the Apostles," does not accurately describe the contents of the book but is the kind of title used at that time by Hellenistic (Greek) historical writers. Other books from the period have similar names, for instance, "Acts of Hannibal" and "Acts of Alexander."

The book gives the history of the beginning of the Christian church. It covers approximately thirty years from shortly after the resurrection of Christ to around AD 65. It does not give a total or broad history. Luke was careful to limit what he said to what he could personally check out. He did not tell about all the apostles nor about churches that were being started in such places as Egypt and possibly India. He did not even tell about the beginning of the church at Rome. Christianity is rich, however, because of what he did tell. His book is the only authentic existing record of the early church years. Not only is the book important because it provides information about the first churches, but it also provides a framework for the rest of the New Testament.

The theme of Acts is found in 1:8—"But you shall receive power when the Holy

128

Spirit has come upon you; and you shall be my witnesses in Jerusalem and in all Judea and Samaria and to the end of the earth." The book follows the progressive stages stated in that verse. The Holy Spirit came upon a group of people in Jerusalem. The Christian church began that day in Jerusalem, then spread into Judea and Samaria, then reached out into all settled areas of the world. The stages are given as follows:

Acts 1—2   The beginning of the Christian church
Acts 3—7   The early church in Jerusalem and the beginning of its organizational structure
Acts 8—12   The extension of the church into Judea and Samaria, then north along the Mediterranean coast and west to the island of Cyprus
Acts 13—28   The expansion of the church across Turkey, into Greece, and finally into Italy.

Although the main purpose of the book was to give an account of the early years of Christian progress, the writing accomplished a secondary goal. The work is an apology for Christianity, that is, it is a book in defense of the Christian faith. It shows that the church did not deserve to be persecuted or criticized. It was not a destructive organization but one that offered only good to individuals and to nations.

Two men stand out in the Book of Acts. The first is Jesus' disciple Peter who is the leading individual told about in chapters 1—12. The rest of the book mainly concerns the work of Paul (Saul in Hebrew), a devout Jew who wanted to eradicate Christianity before a dramatic experience made him its strongest supporter. There is some overlapping of the two sections, however. Paul is prominent in chapter 9, Peter, in chapter 15.

The section emphasizing Peter (chs. 1—12) covers the earliest days of the Christian church. The church was "born" on the Jewish religious holiday of Pentecost (for a discussion of Pentecost see discussion of the Book of Exodus in this book) when a group of Jesus' disciples and friends met together and were suddenly filled with the Holy Spirit. They went out into the streets telling of "the mighty works of God" (Acts 2:11). The public immediately reacted to what they heard; some believed, others ridiculed. The section continues with the early successes and problems of the church both within the fellowship that was formed and without it in the larger world. Because of the reaction of Jewish religious leaders, the early Christians faced arrests, beatings, and death. Within the fellowship itself difficulties arose as people struggled to give up customs and prejudices they had always held. The first church officers (Acts 6)—men to "serve tables" (possibly deacons)—were selected to meet a controversy: Hellenists said Jewish widows received provisions from the church while their widows were neglected (6:1). It took a vision and the faith of Cornelius, a Gentile, to cause Peter to learn with surprise that Christianity was meant for Gentiles as well as Jews (Acts 10). A council meeting of church leaders was held before early Christians agreed that Gentile Christians did not have to submit to Jewish traditions such as circumcision (Acts 15).

The section emphasizing Paul (Acts 13—28) covers the first period of the church's missionary outreach. Paul and Barnabas were the first people sent out from a church for the express purpose of teaching about Christ and for establishing new churches. Paul exerted a remarkable influence on Christianity. Brilliant, educated, indefatigable, he survived shipwrecks, riots, repeated beatings, and imprisonments. He intrigued kings, fascinated scholars, and won the loyalty of soldiers who guarded him when he was a prisoner.

Paul's missionary journeys form an important part of the book. He made three. The first was a circular trip from Antioch to Cyprus and to several cities in southern Turkey. The second journey took him into Greece where he established such churches as the ones in Philippi, Thessalonica, and Corinth. The third trip covered the same general area as the second. Later Paul was taken to Rome for trial and that trip proved to be as much a missionary journey as the ones planned for the purpose.

The record of Paul's journeys as given in Acts is especially important because of the background it provides for understanding the letters in the rest of the New Testament. The letters allow us to glimpse the inner life of early churches, but without Acts we would lack any knowledge of how those churches were formed.

Daily Bible Reading Schedule

Week 36
Acts 1
Acts 2
Acts 3
Acts 4
Acts 5
Acts 6
Acts 7 to 8:1

Week 37
Acts 9:1-30
Acts 10
Acts 11:1-26
Acts 12
Acts 13:1-3, 49 to 14:7
Acts 15
Acts 19:21-41

Week 38
Acts 21:17-34
Acts 22:30 to 23:11
Acts 23:12-35
Acts 24
Acts 25:1-12
Acts 25:13-27
Acts 26:1-23

Week 39
Acts 26:24-32
Acts 27:1-12
Acts 27:13-26
Acts 27:27-44
Acts 28:1-10
Acts 28:11-22
Acts 28:23-31

Suggested Topics for Further Research

Caesarea: seaport where Paul was taken for trial
Felix and Festus: procurators under whom Paul was a prisoner
Stephen: first Christian martyr
Baptism: ceremony of initiation into the church
Lord's Supper: service in memory of Christ
Ordinance: ceremonies used in the churches as baptism and the Lord's Supper
Herod's Temple: magnificent Temple in Jerusalem
Fortress Antonia: Roman fort built in one corner of the Temple wall

Reinforce Your Memory

Which three Gospels are called Synoptic? Why? What is different about the other Gospel?

What do the Gospels tell? What is their primary aim?

What does Acts do? Who are the principal people told about in Acts?

The _____ Empire was in power during the time of the New Testament. _____ _____ was emperor at the time of Christ's birth.

List differences in the Pharisees and the Sadducees.

When Herod the Great died, three of his sons became _____. Herod Philip ruled the _____ portion of the land his father had ruled. Herod Archelaus ruled three areas, _____, _____, and _____. Herod Antipas ruled two areas, _____ and _____.

Herod Archelaus was replaced by a _____. In the Gospels the most important procurator was _____.

In the space below draw a map of the Roman Empire showing the territory of the Jews and its divisions. Show the routes Paul took on his missionary journeys.

SECTION **6**

Literature of the New Testament

The last twenty-two books in the New Testament are like the last twenty-two books in the Old Testament in that they contain writings that developed as a result of the events told about in the preceding books. Mostly the writing consists of letters. Some were written to individuals; some were written to churches.

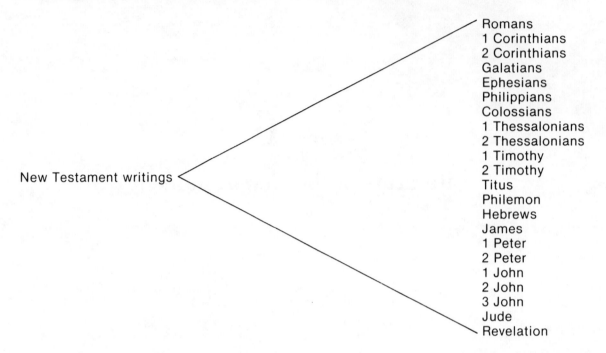

New Testament writings

Romans
1 Corinthians
2 Corinthians
Galatians
Ephesians
Philippians
Colossians
1 Thessalonians
2 Thessalonians
1 Timothy
2 Timothy
Titus
Philemon
Hebrews
James
1 Peter
2 Peter
1 John
2 John
3 John
Jude
Revelation

Many of the letters were written to solve problems in the early churches. There were problems with syncretism—people trying to blend Christianity with other religions. There were organizational problems—what kind of person should serve as a preacher or a deacon. There were problems with expression—people didn't know how to explain Christianity to others.

The titles that have been given to the letters represent either the place or person to whom each letter was written, or the name of the person who wrote the letter. For instance 1 and 2 Corinthians were written by Paul to the church at Corinth, Greece; Titus was written by Paul to an individual named Titus; and Jude was written by an individual named Jude, "brother of James" (v. 1).

Reading the letters is like hearing one side of a telephone conversation. Some statements are easy to understand, and others unclear because we do not know the details about what is being discussed. Much that would be unclear, however, is not hard to understand because of information given in Acts. The Book of Acts tells about many of the churches and individuals to whom the letters were addressed, or by whom they were written.

The last book in the New Testament, Revelation, is very different from the other books. It is not a letter but a book written in apocalyptic form similar to that used in parts of the Old Testament Books of Ezekiel, Daniel, and Zechariah. The style of writing was very popular at the time of the New Testament. Revelation describes scenes that are not bound by the usual sense of time or natural laws, but the teaching is in keeping with the rest of the Bible. It shows that the righteousness of God will ultimately be fully seen, and both the just and unjust will receive their due.

Chart 20.
Romans through 2 Thessalonians

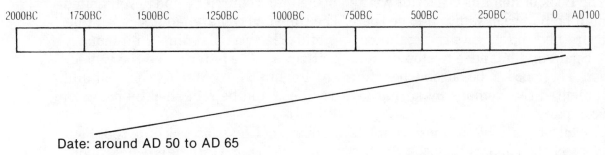

2000BC   1750BC   1500BC   1250BC   1000BC   750BC   500BC   250BC   0   AD100

Date: around AD 50 to AD 65

Genesis
Exodus
Leviticus
Numbers
Deuteronomy
Joshua
Judges
Ruth
1 Samuel
2 Samuel
1 Kings
2 Kings
1 Chronicles
2 Chronicles
Ezra
Nehemiah
Esther
Job
Psalms
Proverbs
Ecclesiastes
Song of Solomon
Isaiah
Jeremiah
Lamentations
Ezekiel
Daniel
Hosea
Joel
Amos
Obadiah
Jonah
Micah
Nahum
Habakkuk
Zephaniah
Haggai
Zechariah
Malachi

Matthew
Mark
Luke
John
Acts
Romans
1 Corinthians
2 Corinthians
Galatians
Ephesians
Philippians
Colossians
1 Thessalonians
2 Thessalonians
1 Timothy
2 Timothy
Titus
Philemon
Hebrews
James
1 Peter
2 Peter
1 John
2 John
3 John
Jude
Revelation

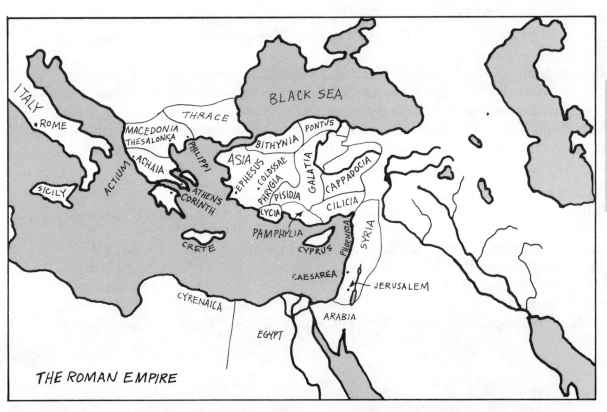

THE ROMAN EMPIRE

Romans

The Book of Romans is a letter written by Paul to a church he had never visited although he had been wanting to go there. The time had come when it seemed that the desire had moved into the realm of possibility. He was planning a missionary trip to Spain and intended to stop in Rome on the way. The letter paved the way for his visit. He hoped to be of some benefit to the Roman church during the visit and complimented the Romans by saying he knew he would be refreshed by being in their company.

The letter contains the most complete summary of Christian teaching that Paul wrote, a fact that makes the book the first great writing on Christian beliefs about God. In it Paul expressed profound and sublime thoughts. He was not, as in most of his letters, dealing with some immediate problem in the church, but writing about the core of faith to people he did not know.

Part of the book applies to any Christian church; part of it was directed specifically to the Roman church. The major portion of the book, excluding the introduction and the conclusion, contains five main divisions.

The first division, in Romans 1—3 (excluding the introduction), concerns the world's need for redemption. In speaking of that need Paul did not talk about poor social conditions, or bad politics, but of the basic problem—willful rejection of truth. Truth, he said, is so obvious from nature that there is no excuse for anyone not to know God.

Paul especially stressed *anyone,* not just Jews. The complacent Jew had no superiority over the non-Jew (Gentile). God shows no partiality. The Jew had the advantage of learning about God but that advantage could not remove his guilt. All people had the same opportunity of being forgiven through Jesus Christ. God sent Christ to make good triumph over evil.

Three key words are used in Paul's explanation:

Justification.—To "declare righteous" or pronounce "not guilty"; opposite of "find guilty," it is God's doing and it means "forgiven and brought into right relationship"

Redemption.—Deliverance, as when God brought his people out of Egypt or when he brought them out of Babylon; yet redemption means deliverance from spiritual, not physical, bondage

Expiation.—Removal of evil infection; not a matter of sacrifice appeasing but of divine love removing the stain; no place for human boasting as only God can break the bondage

The second division, Romans 4, refers to Abraham and shows that the Old Testament teachings harmonize with the New. Abraham was not justified because of working to win God's favor but because of his faith. He trusted God and believed God's promises. The same trait must be exhibited by Christians.

The third division, Romans 5—8, concerns the new kind of life that a Christian leads. It is a life that produces endurance, character, hope. And "hope does not disappoint us, because God's love has been poured into our hearts through the Holy Spirit which has been given to us" (Rom. 5:5). It is a life that, though once enslaved by sin, has "become obedient from the heart to the standard of teaching to which you have been committed" (Rom. 6:17). It is a life in which one knows he has become a child of God because of "the Spirit himself bearing witness with our spirit" (Rom. 8:16).

In the fourth division, Romans 9—11, Paul wrote about his own people, the Jews, and contrasted them with all non-Jews. He wanted to convey the fact that physical lineage does not make a person closer to God, "For there is no distinction between Jew and Greek; the same Lord is Lord of all and bestows his riches upon all who call upon him" (Rom. 10:12). He also wanted to convey that it is the responsibility of people who know the good news of Christ to pass it on to others: "How are they to believe in him of whom they have never heard? And how are they to hear without a preacher? And how can men preach unless they are sent? As it is written, 'How beautiful are the feet of those who preach good news!'" (Rom. 10:14-15).

The fifth section, Romans 12—16, begins by discussing Christian conduct—live in harmony with one another (Rom. 12:16), hold to what is good (Rom. 12:9), respect the government (Rom. 13:1), pay taxes (Rom. 13:7). Then Paul addressed a problem that seemed to arise frequently in churches—some people felt that Christians should not eat certain foods and that certain days were of great importance. Paul did not feel bound by such restrictions but did feel responsible for any actions that might hurt the conscience of someone else. He therefore taught that Christians should never do anything that makes it harder for another person to become a Christian.

1 Corinthians

First Corinthians is a letter written by Paul to the church at Corinth, Greece. Paul had gone to Greece on his second missionary journey (his first in Europe) and had preached in several cities but was forced by jealous Jews to leave one town after another. He finally went to Corinth where, surprisingly, he had much success and stayed in the city for eighteen months.

Paul's success in Corinth was surprising because of the kind of city Corinth was. It was located on a very narrow strip of land connecting the lower section of Greece to the mainland. On each side of the strip there were seaports. The ports were popular because ships could dock at one of them, transfer goods overland to the opposite port, load goods on other ships, and travel on, avoiding the hazardous trip around the southern peninsula. Sailors received their pay at the seaports and many went to Corinth to spend their money. Corinth became the gambling center of the ancient world. The ruins of the city show that around the central square, which was paved with marble, were dozens of shops and entertainment centers.

Acts 18:1-11 gives an account of Paul's first visit to Corinth and of how the church there was organized. After Paul left the city he wrote several letters to the church. First Corinthians is one of the letters. It is an important document not only because of what it teaches but because it gives a vivid picture of an actual church at the time of Paul.

First Corinthians was written to correct problems in the church. The congregation had divided into small groups, each group attaching itself to a different leader. Paul corrected the people saying that they all had been baptized in the name of Christ, not some in the name of Cephas or Apollos or Paul. After correcting them for their factionalism, Paul continued by answering questions they had asked in a letter they had written to him.

The letter has sometimes been called "the layman's charter" because of its presentation of Christian principles. Among the topics Paul addressed are:

Immaturity.—The Corinthians were like babes having to live on milk instead of solid food; jealousy and strife proved their childishness.

Immorality.—Such wrong among church members was like yeast in bread, affecting them all; they needed instead "the unleavened bread of sincerity and truth" (5:8).

Lawsuits.—Christians should be wise enough to settle their own disputes.

Marriage.—Husband and wives should respect each other and should remain together, not separating and divorcing.

Food offered to idols.—Eating such food would not harm the body but if it offended the conscience it should be left alone; also Christians should not eat what offends the conscience of another Christian.

Christian freedom.—Although free, Paul made himself slave to any condition that would win people to Christ; to the weak he showed his weaknesses; to the Jew he showed willingness to obey Jewish laws.

Lord's Supper.—Not a covered dish dinner shared with favorites but a worship experience recognizing what Christ has done.

Spiritual gifts.—Versatile, of all kinds, but all are to be used to build up the church.

Love.—Love is the greatest of all gifts (expressed especially in 1 Cor. 13, perhaps the most beautiful writing in the New Testament).

Tongues.—Christians should strive to be understood lest harm be done to listeners.

Worship.—Use a hymn, a lesson, "Let all things be done for edification" (14:26).

Resurrection.—Christ "was raised" (15:4) giving the Christian assurance that "in Christ shall all be made alive" (15:22); the resurrected body is a spiritual body, "For this perishable nature must put on imperishable, and this mortal nature must put on immortality" (15:53).

2 Corinthians

Paul wrote 2 Corinthians probably about a year after 1 Corinthians. During that year he probably wrote at least one and possibly more letters to the Corinthian church (letters we do not now possess), and he also paid a brief visit to the church. He wanted to visit again but was worried about the Corinthians' reactions to his letters and his visit. He had been severe with them and was afraid they might not have understood his intentions. Because of his fears he sent the young minister Titus to Corinth to find out how the church was getting along. He spent a tense period waiting and was deeply relieved when Titus returned, bringing reassuring news from the church. He then wrote the letter known as 2 Corinthians. It is a moving document with Paul expressing his gratefulness and joy over his reconciliation with the church and his greater joy that "in Christ God was reconciling the world to himself" (5:19).

Second Corinthians can be studied most easily by looking at the consecutive subjects discussed in it. Chapters 1 and 2 give the background for the letter, a description of the anxiety Paul had been experiencing as he waited to hear from the Corinthian church. Chapters 3 through 6 contain the heart of the writing, a detailed discussion of the role of a Christian minister. Chapter 7 refers again to the same fears Paul had mentioned in the beginning of the letter. Chapters 8 and 9 contain an appeal to the Corinthians to donate money for the needy in Jerusalem, a project they had pledged the year before. The final chapters, 10 through 13, contain a great deal of information about Paul. He wrote about himself, not because he thought of himself as an interesting subject but because his own life showed that the things people often brag about fade into insignificance when contrasted with God's power.

The letter is personal. Paul knew the Corinthians too well to speak to them without referring to his own relationship with them. Yet the intimacy of the letter does not make its teachings limited to the Corinthians. Paul's description of a true Christian is as accurate today as it was in his own day. A Christian, Paul said, has been commissioned by God and entrusted with the message of reconciliation.

Paul took up the subject of Christian ministers because certain ministers had been traveling about carrying flattering recommendations with them and preaching with only the goal of putting money in their pockets. Paul said a Christian minister is not a peddler of God's Word, but is an ambassador for Christ who appeals, on behalf of Christ, that listeners be reconciled to God. The letter of recommendation Paul wanted was one written on hearts, not with ink, but with the Spirit of the living God. Such a message can always be known and read by all people through the lives of those on whose hearts it has been written.

In his discussion on donating money to the needy Paul wrote about the attitude that should be in the heart of a giver. A person who gives should do so with gratefulness because of having something to give. One should give in faith, knowing that the God who supplied what one gives is worthy of being trusted to continue to supply one's needs.

Galatians

The letter to the Galatians discusses one major theme—whether or not a Gentile must become a Jew before becoming a Christian. The question had become serious in Galatia, a province in the country presently known as Turkey. The letter is invaluable; it sets forth the principles in Christianity that make it a world religion rather than a branch of Judaism.

Paul wrote that he was astonished that the Galatians had so quickly turned from the gospel he had preached to a different gospel that actually wasn't a gospel at all but a perversion. To illustrate what he was talking about he gave some details of his own conversion and events following it. In so doing he told about some phases of his life that are not told about anywhere else in the Bible. Through telling about his life he was able to convey his point that a Christian does not have to become a Jew before becoming a Christian. After his own conversion some of the early Christian leaders had acted as though it were necessary that a person become a Jew and adopt Jewish customs when they accepted Christ. Paul argued showing that conforming to Jewish ritual could not cleanse a person's heart. If justification came through law "then Christ died to no purpose" (Gal. 2:21), and "if a law had been given which could make alive, then righteousness would indeed be by the law" (Gal. 3:21).

The letter opens with a shorter greeting than Paul normally used, a fact that indicates his anxiety to get to the subject at hand. The main body of the letter, aside from the opening and closing, can be divided into three parts. Chapters 1 and 2 contain Paul's personal reasons for saying Christians do not need to adopt Judaism. Chapters 3 and 4 contain arguments supporting his points. Chapters 5 and 6 contain appeals for Christians to recognize the fruits of evil (Gal. 5:19) and the fruits of righteousness (Gal. 5:22). The production of good fruit is not determined by obeying or not obeying customs and rituals: "For in Christ Jesus neither circumcision nor uncircumcision is of any avail, but faith working through love" (Gal. 5:6).

Ephesians

Ephesians takes its name from Ephesus, an important city that was once located in present-day Turkey. The book is not a personal letter directed specifically to the church at Ephesus but was probably sent there as a central point and copies circulated among a number of churches. The letter is majestic writing that is as modern as the day it was written because of the single subject it addresses. That subject is the church.

The chapters fall into two separate groups of three each. The first three teach what the church is. The second three teach what Christians are to do.

In the first three chapters the church is described as the body and Christ as the head of that body. When Christians come into the church, although they are from many lands and varied backgrounds, they join together in one fellowship in Christ, "For he is our peace, who has made us both one, and has broken down the dividing wall of hostility" (Eph. 2:14). The church was designed to be a union of all believers. Jews with Gentiles "are fellow heirs, members of the same body, and partakers of the promise in Christ Jesus through the gospel" (Eph. 3:5-6).

These chapters also teach the doctrine that has come to be known as the Trinity. It shows God as three in One—the Father who blesses (Eph. 1:3), the Son who redeems (Eph. 1:5-7), and the Spirit who seals belief (Eph. 1:13).

The second three chapters contain pleas that Christians live in unity with God's Spirit and build up the body of Christ (which is the church) and "grow up in every way into him who is the head, into Christ, from whom the whole body, joined and knit together by every joint with which it is supplied, when each part is working properly, makes bodily growth and upbuilds itself in love" (Eph. 4:15-16). To do this Christians must put off their old nature and "be renewed in the spirit of your minds, and put on the new nature, created after the likeness of God in true righteousness and holiness" (Eph. 4:23). Christians must speak the truth, do honest work, say nothing evil, do what builds up, be kind, forgiving, imitators of God. Christians should speak to each other joyously, their hearts should make "melody to the Lord"

140

(Eph. 5:19), and they should give thanks to God for all things. Family relationships should be one of love, work should be done "not in the way of eye-service, as men-pleasers, but as servants of Christ, doing the will of God from the heart" (Eph. 6:6). Christians should, in effect, be clothed with the armor of God in order to stand against evil (see Eph. 6:13-17).

Philippians

Philippians is a letter written by Paul to the Christians at Philippi, a city in Greece that was named for Philip, the father of Alexander the Great. The church was the first that Paul established in Europe.

The letter is the most personal that Paul wrote to a group of people. It is obvious that he knew them well and that he was acquainted with some individual members of the group. The relationship he had with the church was similar to that of a much loved and respected headmaster of a school with the faculty and students. He cared about them deeply, recognized and praised their skills, and at the same time prodded them to develop those skills further.

The letter was written because the church at Philippi had sent a gift to Paul by Epaphroditus, one of its members. Epaphroditus had intended to stay with Paul for a time to help him but had gotten sick and almost died. The Philippians had heard of his illness and were worried about him. Paul wrote the letter and sent it to Philippi by Epaphroditus, so the Philippians could see that Epaphroditus had gotten well.

Philippians is arranged like an ordinary friendly letter. Topics are mentioned as they come to mind. The letter is sometimes spoken of as the joy letter because the words *joy* and *rejoice* are repeated so frequently in it, more than in any other of Paul's letters. The expression of joy is significant because Paul was in prison possibly facing death.

Joy, however, is not the only emphasis of the letter. Paul was concerned because self-centeredness had produced an unhealthy spirit in the church. To point out the problem and to help eliminate it Paul spoke in his letter of people who had displayed examples of self-sacrifice: Christ, Timothy, Epaphroditus, Paul himself.

Paul identified with the Philippians. He knew they faced trials similar to his own. Yet he rejoiced because problems had created means of spreading the gospel. Even Paul's imprisonment had served several good purposes, among them a way for the Praetorian guards (Caesar's special forces) to learn of Christ.

It is obvious from the letter that the Philippians had more than once contributed financially to Paul which was an unusual thing for a church to do. Ordinarily he worked for his living. As he wrote he expressed his appreciation for the gifts but more importantly for the fruitfulness they showed in their lives by being willing to give.

Sandwiched between his compliments of their maturity and generosity Paul inserted advice. His main concern was that they have unity in Christ and "stand firm in one spirit, with one mind striving side by side for the faith of the gospel" (Phil. 1:27). Paul recommended the example of Christ (Phil. 2:5-11) in one of the greatest passages in the New Testament. Some were grumbling and fussing. In guiding them Paul spoke not only about the disturbances this discord was creating, but he addressed two practical individual problems: anxiety and thinking. Anxiety could be met by taking requests to God, but they were to do it with thanksgiving. And thoughts should be consciously controlled. People should put into the mind what is good and worth praising. "Finally, brethren, whatever is true, whatever is honorable, whatever is just, whatever is pure, whatever is lovely, whatever is gracious, if there is any excellence, if there is anything worthy of praise, think about these things" (Phil. 4:8).

Colossians

The letter to the Colossians is similar in form to the letter to the Ephesians. It follows the same pattern with the first chapters on what to believe and the latter chapters on how to act. Yet the two letters were written for different purposes. Ephesians was written to teach, Colossians was written to combat heresy.

Like Ephesus, Colossae was in what is present-day Turkey. A Christian church had been organized in the town and into the church had come people with ideas that blended with Christianity yet distorted it. These ideas taught that certain times, such as the arrival of a new moon, were more sacred than others. They taught that certain rituals, such as circumcision were essential. They taught that certain foods should be avoided, and that angels should be worshiped.

News that these false teachings had infiltrated the Colossian church was carried to Paul by Epaphras, a man who was probably converted to Christianity under Paul's preaching. In response to the news, Paul wrote the letter of Colossians and sent it to the church by Tychicus whom Paul called a "fellow servant in the Lord" (Col. 4:7). Tychicus may also have carried Paul's letter to Philemon since Philemon lived in Colossae.

The theme of the letter is the supremacy and sufficiency of Christ. The letter is short, and it was sent to a small town, yet in teaching the preeminence of Christ it reaches a higher point than all other New Testament books. It teaches that Christ is not one power among many, but the accumulation of all, and Christians are complete in him.

Chapters 1 to 3:4 of the letter are doctrinal. They teach Christian beliefs. The remainder of the letter, chapters 3:5 to 5:18, is practical. It teaches Christian behavior.

Paul was not personally acquainted with the Colossian church, yet he could not allow it to have needs and problems without attempting to help. He wrote to correct those who were damaging the church and to spur church members to look intelligently at the restrictions that were being pushed upon them. "Why do you submit to regulations, 'Do not handle, Do not taste, Do not touch.' . . . These have indeed an appearance of wisdom in promoting rigor of devotion and self-abasement and severity to the body, but they are of no value in checking the indulgence of the flesh" (Col. 2:20-23). As for the worship of angels Paul told them that such ideas came from minds that were "puffed up without reason" (Col. 2:18). Christians should not be deceived but know that Christ is sufficient, "For in him the whole fulness of diety dwells bodily" (Col. 2:9).

Paul appealed to the Colossians to consider the nature of Christianity, telling them that circumcision does not determine the inward attitude of a person, nor does race or social status. Christianity has to do with hearts, with compassion, kindness, patience, with being thankful. It has to do with respect in marriage, with good relationships between parents and children, with the way masters treat slaves.

Although Paul was in prison when he wrote to the Colossians, he did not ask them to pray for his release. Instead he asked that they pray that he might explain Christianity clearly. And his challenge to them was that they too might "know how you ought to answer every one" (Col. 4:6).

1 Thessalonians

The seaport city of Thessalonica (present-day Salonika) was named for the sister of Alexander the Great. At the time of Paul it was the capital of part of Macedonia (northern Greece) and a major trading center. Its main street was part of the Via Egnatia, the principal highway to Rome.

Paul went to Thessalonica on his second missionary journey shortly after being forced to leave Philippi. At Philippi certain Jews had Paul beaten and put in jail. They did not like the fact that Paul's preaching attracted the God-fearers, people who had been interested in Judaism because of its teaching about God. They wanted to hear Paul because he preached about the God of the Jews but did not teach Jewish ritual and ceremony. The Jews became angry and had Paul arrested. City officials soon released him but ordered him to leave the city. He went to Thessalonica where he preached for several weeks but was forced to leave because of the same kind of problems he had experienced at Philippi. (Acts 17:1-10 records Paul's stay in Thessalonica.)

Sometime later Paul sent his young assistant, Timothy, to Thessalonica to see whether the few weeks' work he had done there had prospered at all. Timothy brought back the good news that the Christians in Thessalonica were being faithful. In his thanksgiving over the news, Paul wrote the letter known as 1 Thessalonians.

Paul's chief purpose in writing was to express his joy that, despite obstacles, Christianity was progressing in Thessalonica, but he took the opportunity to address some other topics. First, he defended his own character showing that he did not deserve complaints some Jews had made against him. Next, he encouraged them to live a pure moral life. And last, he took up two questions that evidently Timothy had told him were worrying the Thessalonians. They were concerned about whether Christians who died before Christ's second coming would get a share in the blessing. And they were concerned about just when the second coming would take place.

Paul answered that the righteous who died before Christ's coming would share in the coming just as the ones who were still living. As for the time of Christ's coming, Christians should always be ready. Yet they should not sit and wait but should do as the Thessalonians themselves were already doing, "encourage one another and build one another up" (1 Thess. 5:11).

2 Thessalonians

Second Thessalonians was written shortly after 1 Thessalonians, and the two letters are very much alike. A new problem had developed, however, that needed attention. Some people had the idea that the Day of the Lord had already come. There were rumors that Paul had written a letter telling about it. Paul refuted the idea. He said he had not written anything to that effect, and he did not want them to become confused by that or other false teachings that were circulating.

The Day of the Lord, Paul said, would not come until after certain things had taken place. Lawlessness was already at work, but it would become much worse. Paul spoke of a "lawless one" who would oppose all religion and objects pertaining to religion. He would take his seat in the Temple announcing that he was God. Under his leadership lawlessness would become extreme, and many people would be deceived by him. But Christians who love the truth would not. Paul told them that they did not need to worry because they had been "saved through sanctification by the Spirit and belief in the truth" (2 Thess. 2:13).

Paul then addressed the subject of the second coming that he had discussed in 1 Thessalonians. Some were using it as an excuse to stop working. They were waiting in idleness. Paul firmly denounced such an attitude: "If anyone will not work, let him not eat" (2 Thess. 3:10). But people who are confused in such a way should not be looked upon as enemies. Instead they should be warned.

Daily Bible Reading Schedule

Week 40
Rom. 2
Rom. 3
Rom. 4
Rom. 5
Rom. 11
Rom. 12
Rom. 14

Week 41
1 Cor. 2
1 Cor. 6
1 Cor. 12
1 Cor. 13
1 Cor. 14
1 Cor. 15
1 Cor. 16

Week 42
2 Cor. 2
2 Cor. 3
2 Cor. 4
2 Cor. 5
2 Cor. 8
2 Cor. 11:1-15
2 Cor. 11:16-33

Week 43
Gal. 1
Gal. 2
Gal. 3:1-18
Gal. 3:19 to 4:7
Gal. 4:8-31
Gal. 5
Gal. 6

Week 44
Eph. 1
Eph. 2
Eph. 3
Eph. 4:1-16
Eph. 4:17-32
Eph. 5
Eph. 6

Week 45
Phil. 1
Phil. 2
Phil. 3
Col. 1
Col. 2
Col. 3:1-17
Col. 3:18 to 4:18

Week 46
1 Thess. 1
1 Thess. 2
1 Thess. 3:1 to 4:12
1 Thess. 4:13 to 5
2 Thess. 1
2 Thess. 2
2 Thess. 3

Suggested Topics for Further Study

Rome: capital of the Roman Empire
Corinth: city in Greece
Galatia: province in area presently known as Turkey
Ephesus: ancient city that was once in Turkey
Philippi: city in Greece
Thessalonica: city in Greece
Praetorian guard: Caesar's special forces

Reinforce Your Memory

Think over the major purpose of each of Paul's letters to churches. List an important idea from each of them.

Romans

1 Corinthians

2 Corinthians

Galatians

Ephesians

Philippians

Colossians

1 Thessalonians

2 Thessalonians

In the space below draw a map of the Roman Empire and locate the cities and provinces to which the letters were directed.

Chart 21.
1 Timothy through Revelation

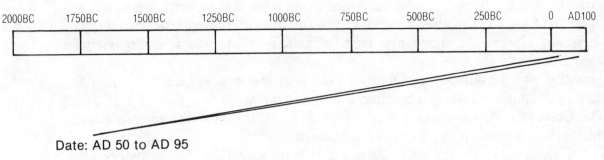

2000BC 1750BC 1500BC 1250BC 1000BC 750BC 500BC 250BC 0 AD100

Date: AD 50 to AD 95

Genesis
Exodus
Leviticus
Numbers
Deuteronomy
Joshua
Judges
Ruth
1 Samuel
2 Samuel
1 Kings
2 Kings
1 Chronicles
2 Chronicles
Ezra
Nehemiah
Esther
Job
Psalms
Proverbs
Ecclesiastes
Song of Solomon
Isaiah
Jeremiah
Lamentations
Ezekiel
Daniel
Hosea
Joel
Amos
Obadiah
Jonah
Micah
Nahum
Habakkuk
Zephaniah
Haggai
Zechariah
Malachi

Matthew
Mark
Luke
John
Acts
Romans
1 Corinthians
2 Corinthians
Galatians
Ephesians
Philippians
Colossians
1 Thessalonians
2 Thessalonians
1 Timothy
2 Timothy
Titus
Philemon
Hebrews
James
1 Peter
2 Peter
1 John
2 John
3 John
Jude
Revelation

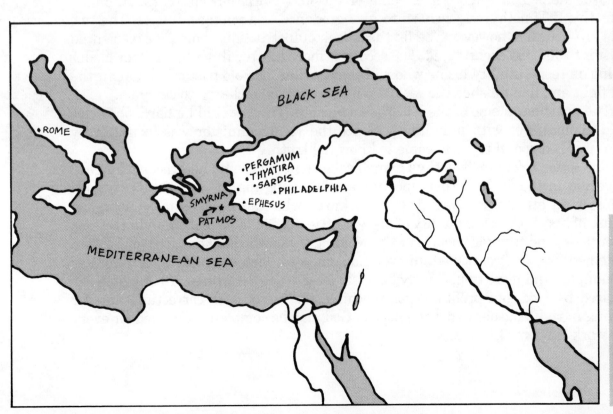

BLACK SEA

ROME

PERGAMUM
THYATIRA
SARDIS
PHILADELPHIA
SMYRNA
PATMOS
EPHESUS

MEDITERRANEAN SEA

1 Timothy

First Timothy, 2 Timothy, and Titus are three New Testament letters that are known as the Pastoral Epistles. The books are the first known instructions written for Christian clergymen. They are from a mature pastor to less experienced associate pastors.

Timothy was a youthful associate of Paul and was a great help to the older minister. Paul spoke of him as a brother, a son, a fellow worker.

The Book of 1 Timothy has a dual purpose. First, it gives guidance in church administration. Second, it opposes harmful teaching.

In the category of church administration it gives directions for ministers; they should study and understand what they are to teach. It gives instruction for worship services; they should be times of prayer, not of bickering or displaying fancy clothing and jewelry. It tells that the lives of church leaders should demonstrate their worthiness; they should manage their own families well, should be skilled in handling the tasks they are selected to do, should be sensible and gentle. It tells what kind of attitudes should be held toward various groups in the church, toward the young, old, widows, leaders, and slaves.

In the category of harmful teaching, the letter speaks against people who argue over words and have "a morbid craving for controversy" (1 Tim. 6:4) but are unacquainted with truth. They want to learn of God just because they think it might help them financially. They aren't concerned with the contentment godliness brings; they have "what is falsely called knowledge" (1 Tim. 6:20), but "have missed the mark as regards the faith" (1 Tim. 6:21).

2 Timothy

Like 1 Timothy, the Book of 2 Timothy is named for the youthful associate of Paul who helped in the work of some of the first Christian churches. And like 1 Timothy, 2 Timothy was written to give guidance to a young minister. The two books are not alike however. The first is a book of instructions from an experienced minister to one less experienced. The second is more like a will with the older leader passing on responsibility to one who will replace him. The old pastor had fought the good fight and had finished the race; the new was given a charge to carry on.

The principal theme of the letter is endurance. Times would be hard, obstacles would abound, but with unfailing patience the young minister was to use every means at his disposal to lead people to know the truth.

The letter refers to Timothy's home background where he had received a good foundation in the faith. It then encouraged the young man to endure like a good soldier or an athlete. He was to be a workman who had no need to be ashamed because of his effort or the quality of his work. He needed to be mature in his actions and outlook, and to guide people gently, avoiding those who held to a form of religion but denied the power of it. Paul himself had endured; Timothy could look to him as an example. And more importantly he could look to the Scriptures, all of which are "inspired by God and profitable for teaching, for reproof, for correction, and for training in righteousness, that the man of God may be complete, equipped for every good work" (2 Tim. 3:16-17).

Titus

Titus, like Timothy, was a young co-worker of Paul. He is mentioned in several of Paul's letters although not as often as Timothy; therefore, not as much is known about him.

The letter directed to Titus was written for essentially the same purpose as 1 Timothy, that is, to help regulate the organization of churches and to help churches avoid harmful teachings.

Titus contains three main topics, one in each of its three chapters. Chapter 1 explains what is required of church leaders. Chapter 2 speaks of the proper way to treat particular groups of people in the church—older women, younger men, slaves. Chapter 3 discusses right and wrong conduct—avoid hate and fussing, show meekness and gentleness, remember that "we ourselves were once foolish, disobedient, led astray, slaves to various passions and pleasures, passing our days in malice and envy, hated by men and hating one another, but when the goodness and loving kindness of God our Savior appeared, he saved us, not because of deeds done by us in righteousness, but in virtue of his own mercy" (Titus 3:3-5).

Philemon

Philemon is a short letter written by Paul to Philemon, a man Paul had never met. The letter was written because Paul had become acquainted with Onesimus, a slave who belonged to Philemon but who had run away. Under Paul's influence Onesimus had become a Christian, and out of his newfound respect for what is right wanted to return to his master. Because Philemon was also a Christian, Paul wrote to him explaining the change in Onesimus and asking Philemon to treat the returning slave as a brother in Christ.

In the Roman Empire at the time of Paul slavery was an accepted institution. The number of slaves was so great that free people feared slaves might unite against them; therefore, laws controlling slaves were extremely severe. Cruelty to slaves was neither questioned nor criticized. Slaves were things, not human beings. They were the property of their masters, were sold like farm animals, and were thought of in the same light.

Paul's appeal that Philemon treat Onesimus as a brother was not only an appeal for one person but essentially an appeal that Christ's love be brought to bear on slavery. It incorporated the principle that had the power to abolish slavery altogether.

Hebrews

Hebrews is considered a letter but is more like a written sermon. It is too long, however, to fit the modern definition of a sermon and may be several progressive sermons carefully put together. The work is a masterpiece of Christian prose, rhythmical and eloquent. It contains a lengthy argument, the most sustained found in any book in the Bible. It is systematically arranged and moves forward step by step. It concentrates on only one subject, that Christianity is superior to Judaism.

Who wrote the book, and when, is not known. It is certain only that it is addressed to Jewish Christians who had become fearful that Christianity did not offer as much as Judaism. Traditions and customs associated with Judaism were so ingrained in them that they believed the traditions offered religious benefits not found in Christianity. They were beginning to wonder if they had made a mistake by giving up their former religion.

They needed assurance. They needed explanations that would help them know they had not given up, but had advanced.

Because of their background the original readers had a good knowledge of the Old Testament, therefore the writer of Hebrews used numerous experiences from it. For this reason the Book of Hebrews is best understood by modern readers who are thoroughly familiar with the Old Testament.

In his argument the writer showed the superiority of Christianity first by comparing Christ with the prophets. The prophets were important because to them God revealed his messages, and they spoke those messages to people. But Christ has more than a message; "He reflects the glory of God and bears the very stamp of his nature" (Heb. 1:3). He compared Christ with the angels who were messengers of God but God crowned Christ "with glory and honor,/putting everything in subjection under his feet" (Heb. 2:7). He compared Christ with Moses the greatest of all Israelite leaders, but in comparison Moses "was faithful in all God's house as a servant" (Heb. 3:5) while Christ "was faithful over God's house as a son" (Heb. 3:6).

Continuing his argument the writer took up the subject of the Levitical priesthood and of sacrifice. He showed that Jesus came as the perfect priest and that all the traditional items associated with the Jewish religion were but shadows representing the true forms that were to come, and did come, through Jesus. Even the law was but a shadow. It offered instructions that people could learn, but the new covenant of Christ altered the inside of a person so that the laws of God were written on their hearts. Sacrifices too were symbolic, representing the need of people to have sins forgiven. Christ came as an everlasting sacrifice offering "the new and living way" (Heb. 10:19).

As the next step in the argument the writer presented a discussion on faith listing one Old Testament personality after another who demonstrated faith (Heb. 11). The people he named were ones who did not have the advantage of seeing what God had done through Christ, yet they believed that such would take place. Their faith gave them "the assurance of things hoped for, the conviction of things not seen" (Heb. 11:1).

The final chapters of the book contain pleas for Christians to look "to Jesus the pioneer and perfecter of our faith" (Heb. 12:2) and to do the things in keeping with a righteous Christian life: strive for peace, show hospitality to strangers, let marriage be held in honor, offer up a sacrifice of praise to God.

James

James is a sermon written like a letter. It is not addressed to just one congregation but to a wide audience.

The letter takes up many different subjects on practical behavior. It is an appeal for Christians to recognize that Christianity has moral demands and for them to assume the responsibility of their profession in Christ. Faith and works go together.

A Christian must step out into society and become involved in a dedicated struggle against injustice, prejudice, immorality. In the process of becoming involved, if anyone "lacks wisdom, let him ask God, who gives to all men generously and without reproaching, and it will be given him. But let him ask in faith, with no doubting" (Jas. 1:5-6a).

The teaching of the letter is similar to the teaching Jesus gave in the Sermon on the Mount. The theme centers around the statement, "be doers of the word, and not hearers only" (Jas. 1:22).

The diversified topics make the letter difficult to outline, yet it is easy to read, and the points are clear. Because the emphasis is on works the letter has sometimes been interpreted as being in conflict with Paul's teaching on faith, yet the two were different only in the fact that they taught different stages of the same thing. When Paul taught that Christians are justified through faith, not by works, he was emphasizing the beginning stage. Justification is not achieved through human effort but through faith in Christ. When James emphasized works, he was speaking of the natural outgrowth of faith. Faith isn't a dead thing, but growing and living, therefore it shows itself through actions. Faith is demonstrated through conduct.

The subject James discussed at most length is the central topic of chapter 3, the tongue. Although a little member of the body, the tongue possesses great power, and no human can tame it.

The concluding subject is on prayer by individuals and by groups of Christians. Prayer has tremendous effect, therefore James encouraged its use in every situation in life, the happy as well as the demanding.

1 Peter

First Peter is a letter from the apostle Peter to several groups of Christians who were being persecuted. The letter has two themes. One concerns being faithful to Christ during times of suffering. The other concerns good behavior.

When persecuted, Christians should remember that Christ suffered and left an example. Christians should follow in his steps. "For what credit is it, if when you do wrong and are beaten for it you take it patiently? But if when you do right and suffer for it you take it patiently, you have God's approval" (1 Pet. 2:20).

In daily living Christians should behave in such a way that others cannot speak of them as wrongdoers but will praise God for the good deeds they see being done. The letter exhorts Christians to so live that others may even be won to Christ through their actions and attitudes. But Christians are to do more than live their faith; they are to learn to talk about it effectively. "Always be prepared to make a defense to any one who calls you to account for the hope that is in you, yet do it with gentleness and reverence" (1 Pet. 3:15).

Because the letter is a teaching letter instructing Christians on behavior, some scholars have suggested that perhaps the middle section was first used as a sermon delivered to newly baptized Christians. It could have been used repeatedly to emphasize the responsibilities of Christians to do well in whatever role they have in life—as citizens under authority of rulers, as husband or wife, as slave or master, as younger or older.

2 Peter

Second Peter was written for two purposes. One was to warn Christians against false teachers. The other was to help Christians stop worrying because the time of Christ's second coming had not yet arrived.

The people to whom the letter was sent needed some spiritual rebuilding. They needed to recognize that although faith is the starting point for Christians, they are never to stop advancing in knowledge or action. If they do, they open themselves to false teaching and are not able to recognize destructive heresies. Such false teachers are like "waterless springs" (2 Pet. 2:17) and they "entice unsteady souls" (2 Pet. 2:14). They promise freedom, "but they themselves are slaves of corruption" (2 Pet. 2:19).

Against such the writer of 2 Peter wanted to protect Christians; therefore, he urged them to advance in Christian growth. The same sort of growth would also ease their minds about the second coming of Christ.

Many Christians had been expecting the second coming momentarily for so long that they had grown tense and anxious. Their anxiety had affected them as adversely as the false teachers had affected them. They needed to learn that the Lord does not view time as we do. God was delaying Christ's coming because he was patiently waiting for people to repent. The letter of 2 Peter advised them that instead of being apprehensive they should be actively living "lives of holiness and godliness" (2 Pet. 3:11). Because you know beforehand that the ignorant take what is hard to understand and twist it, the letter told them, you should "beware lest you be carried away with the error of lawless men and lose your own stability" (2 Pet. 3:17).

1 John

First John is usually classed as a letter although it does not follow the customary form. It contains no greeting or closing, the persons to whom it is addressed are unknown, and the author is not named. Still the book contains internal marks of a letter such as "I am writing to you, little children" (1 John 2:12), and may have been a circulatory epistle passed among several churches.

The writing is so kin to the Gospel of John that there can be little doubt that the same author wrote both books. The words used, and the manner of expression, are very similar in style. The purpose of the two writings is different, however. The Gospel of John was written "that you may believe that Jesus is the Christ, the Son of God, and that believing you may have life in his name" (John 20:31). First John was written to people who already believed but needed strengthening.

First John contains the word *love* more than any other book in the Bible. It particularly teaches that "God is love" (1 John 4:16). The writing was obviously directed to people for whom the author had great affection. He wrote to build up their faith and to warn them against false teachers.

The false teaching that was doing the most harm to Christianity at the time was gnosticism, a religion that was based on knowledge *(gnōsis)*. It claimed to be true Christianity and taught that each person has a divine spark that needs to be released. To achieve release a person could follow one of two modes of life. In one the person lived as an extreme ascetic, denying physical needs and desires. In the other the person lived as a total experimenter, doing anything and denying moral demands. They did not teach kindness and love for one's fellow human beings but only release from all of life's concerns. In contrast 1 John teaches that doing right and having love in one's heart is proof that God's nature has entered a person: "Whoever does not do right is not of God, nor he who does not love his brother" (1 John 3:10).

Jesus himself had warned against false prophets and had told how his followers could recognize them: "You will know them by their fruits. Are grapes gathered from thorns, or figs from thistles? So, every sound tree bears good fruit, but the bad tree bears evil fruit" (Matt. 7:16-17). Throughout 1 John the writer gave similar tests so that those to whom he wrote could determine the difference in Christianity and heresy. (See 1 John 2:9,23; 4:2-3.)

2 John

Second John is a short letter written by the author of 1 John to "the elect lady and her children," probably a phrase that refers to a particular church and its members. He knew the group well. Although the letter is much briefer than 1 John, the main teaching is the same—love the truth and follow it. In addition there is a warning about people who might visit the group and ask to teach. Christians should find out what such people teach before allowing them to stay in their homes or to speak before them. Those teaching the doctrines of Christ should be supported. Anyone teaching other doctrines should be avoided, "for he who greets him shares in his wicked work" (v. 11).

3 John

Third John is a short letter to Gaius, a member of a Christian church where he was evidently a leader with influence. The letter written to him was by the author of 1 and 2 John and is the only one of John's writings addressed to a single individual.

In Gaius' church a person named Diotrephes was usurping authority and creating disharmony. John wrote to compliment Gaius for his good work and to encourage him to continue in it. Expressed in the letter also is the same central idea found in 1 and 2 John: "Beloved, do not imitate evil but imitate good. He who does good is of God; he who does evil has not seen God" (v. 11).

Jude

The letter of Jude was written to warn a church about three things. First, it warned against false teachers. Such teachers were creating division in the church and were walking "in the way of Cain" (v. 11). Second, it warned that there will be a judgment. The ungodly will be convicted, the "grumblers, malcontents, following their own passions, loud-mouthed boasters, flattering people to gain advantage" (v. 16). And third, it warned the church to remain faithful. By staying within the teachings of Christ they might "convince some, who doubt; save some, by snatching them out of the fire" (v. 23).

The letter ends with a short doxology.

Revelation

Revelation is the most difficult book in the New Testament because it is filled with symbolism the meaning of which is not easy to discover. It begins and ends like a letter, but the main body of the book is a drama belonging to the apocalyptic form of literature.

At the time the book was written apocalyptic writing had been popular for several centuries. It was easily understood by those to whom it was addressed but obscure to others. It was used in times of persecution so that its message could be grasped by those for whom it was intended but hidden from others.

The apocalyptic style is always symbolic. The meaning is not direct and literal but such things as numbers, animals, and colors are used to represent points and ideas. Because we today do not know the exact meanings of the symbols the book is not always clear. Daniel provides the best example of apocalyptic writing in the Old Testament. A study of it helps make Revelation clearer because similar symbolisms are used in both books.

The author of Revelation was John. Some think the writer of the Gospel of John wrote Revelation. Others do not. The date of the writing was probably around AD 95 during the reign of Domitian. Earlier Nero had persecuted Christians, but Domitian was the first Roman emperor to inflict wide and intense persecution. He did not single out Christians but considered any one who did not worship Roman gods, and such gods included the emperor himself, as atheists. According to his definition, Christians were atheists, and he ordered that all atheists be either killed or banished to remote areas. John was banished to the rocky island of Patmos where he wrote the Book of Revelation.

The book can be divided into four uneven parts. The first is the introduction in chapter 1. The second, in chapters 2—3, contains seven letters to seven different churches in Asia. The third, chapter 4 through 22:5, is the major portion of the book. It contains a series of dramas—scenes of heaven and angels, of vast areas of the earth, of beasts, plagues, battles, fire, stars. The scenes are augmented with voices and songs, with trumpets and harps. The dramas are so encompassing that they seem to include all time, all events, all purpose. The final section of the book, chapter 22:6-21, is a concluding summary. It follows the preceding sections like the silence that sometimes occurs after a play that has so awed its viewers they must catch their breaths before breaking into tumultuous applause, a moment for assimilating what has come before.

Scholars interpret the Book of Revelation in a variety of ways. The three most popular ways are:

1. It was directed primarily to people living at the time it was written and they understood its code.
2. It was written to foretell the future.
3. It was written to teach spiritual truths to any generation.

Those who view the book as directed to people of its own day believe the apocalyptic form was chosen because of Domitian's persecutions. They see the book as teaching that present troubles are not permanent troubles. God is in control, and his justice and mercy will win in the end.

Those who see the book as having been written to foretell the future believe that the symbolic words represent specific events and persons yet to come. They search to find clues that will help them determine exactly when and where other historical happenings will occur and just how much will take place before the world comes to an end.

Those who see the book as teaching spiritual truths believe that the symbols do not predict specific events but dangers and trials that come repeatedly. They see it as a book that speaks of the future, not because they find clues for naming a Napoleon or a Hitler but because while the present order of events occur good and evil will ever come into conflict. People must choose one side or the other. But evil cannot win; its power has already been broken by Christ.

The dramas in Revelation present more than language can portray. They rise in crescendo giving a message about good overcoming evil, of water without price being freely dispensed, of a time when there will be a new heaven and a new earth. They tell of a city that will have no need of a temple or a sun or a moon "for its temple is the Lord God the Almighty and the Lamb. . . . The glory of God is its light, and its lamp is the Lamb. By its light shall the nations walk; and the kings of the earth shall bring their glory into it, and its gates shall never be shut by day—and there shall be no night there; they shall bring into it the glory and the honor of nations. But nothing unclean shall enter it, nor any one who practices abomination or falsehood, but only those who are written in the Lamb's book of life" (Rev. 21:22-27).

The book is a balanced close for the Scriptures because just as the beginning of Genesis incorporated the whole world and all peoples, so Revelation embraces as wide a scope. And as Genesis reached back to the beginning of all earthly things, so Revelation projects toward end times.

Though people differ greatly in their theories of some parts of the book, most agree that a single theme runs through it—that God is in control, and all people will be judged by his crystal pure righteousness. Those who measure up will be rewarded; those who do not will be punished, but the key to becoming pure is through the acceptance by faith of the Lamb of God, Jesus Christ.

Countless poems, songs, and artistic works have been inspired by the Book of Revelation. As is typical of biblical writings, it prompts a response in the heart, even if not fully understood.

Daily Bible Reading Schedule

Week 47
1 Tim. 1:1-17
1 Tim. 3:1-13
1 Tim. 6:6-20
2 Tim. 2:1-15
2 Tim. 2:20-26
Titus 3:1-11
Philem.

Week 48
Heb. 1:1-14
Heb. 2:1-18
Heb. 3:1-19
Heb. 4:1-16
Heb. 5:1-14
Heb. 6:1-20
Heb. 7:1-28

Week 49
Heb. 8:1-13
Heb. 9:1-14
Heb. 9:15-28
Heb. 10:1-18
Heb. 11:1-39
Heb. 12:1-14
Heb. 13:1-21

Week 50
Jas. 1:1-18
Jas. 1:19-27
Jas. 2:1-13
Jas. 2:14-26
Jas. 3
Jas. 4
Jas. 5

Week 51
1 Pet. 2:1-25
1 Pet. 3:1-22
1 Pet. 4:1-19
2 Pet. 1:3-21
1 John 1:1 to 2:11
1 John 3
Jude

Week 52
Rev. 1
Rev. 2
Rev. 3
Rev. 20
Rev. 21:1-14
Rev. 21:15-27
Rev. 22

Suggested Topics for Further Research

Josephus: Jewish historian who lived from around AD 37 to AD 95
Patmos: island where John wrote Revelation
Nero: fifth emperor of Rome
Titus: Roman general who destroyed Jerusalem around AD 70
Domitian: emperor of Rome from AD 81 to AD 96; persecuted Christians
Petra: city in Idumaea built by the Nabataean Arabs
Didachē: small manual used in early Christian churches
Eusebius: first church historian

Reinforce Your Memory

What features do 1 Timothy, 2 Timothy, and Titus have in common?

What is the main message of the Book of Hebrews?

Summarize the contents of the letters named for people: James, Peter, John, Jude.

What makes Revelation so different from the other books? What is the single theme that runs through the book?

Draw a timeline marked with the approximate period in which the New Testament letters and Revelation were written.

In the space below draw a map of the Roman Empire. Locate Patmos, and designate the general area of the seven churches named in Revelation 2—3.

Bibliography

(The list below is limited to a few books of the type that could be used as resource material for Bible study groups and/or teachers.)

Background Studies:

Anderson, Bernhard W. *Understanding the Old Testament*. Englewood Cliffs, NJ, 1957. Seminary textbook; excellent teaching of the entire Old Testament.

Bailey, Albert Edward. *Daily Life in Bible Times*. New York, 1943. Contains information about customs in Bible times—city and country life, farming, marriage, etc.

Brooks, D. P. *The Bible: How to Understand and Teach It*. Nashville, 1969. Points up the basic principles of biblical understanding and how they should be applied for the most effective teaching.

Cate, Robert L. *How to Interpret the Bible*. Nashville, 1983. Practical help for communicating the message of the Bible.

Coleman, Lucian E., Jr. *How to Teach the Bible*. A highly readable guide for lay Bible teachers to learn how to study, plan, and motivate in the teaching/learning situation. Offers solid and practical methods for teaching and innovative ways of using them.

Cornfeld, Gaalyahn, ed. *Adam to Daniel* and *Daniel to Paul*. The Macmillan Company, 1961.

Everyday Life in Bible Times and *Greece and Rome*. Two books of modern travel in the lands of the Bible, featuring specific areas. Published by National Geographic Society, 1961.

Frank, Harry Thomas. *Discovering the Biblical World*. Harper & Row, Publishers. An illustrated story of the people, archaeology, history, and landscape of the Bible world.

Jones, Clifford M. *Old Testament Illustrations*. Cambridge, 1971. A small book of photographs, maps, and diagrams of biblical places plus explanations.

Keller, Werner. *The Bible as History* and *The Bible as History in Pictures*. New York, William Morrow and Company. Two books giving information and pictures that help the days of the Bible come to life.

Martin, William C. *These Were God's People*. Story of Israel and early Christians. Uses Scripture, ancient history, religious documents, and archaeological findings to "plunge the average layman into the fascinating world of the Bible."

Our Living Bible. Old Testament section by Michael Avi-Yonah and New Testament section by Emil G. Kraeling. A book of pictures and text relating to the areas of the Bible. McGraw-Hill, 1962.

Bible Commentaries:

The Broadman Bible Commentary. Nashville, Broadman Press. A 12-volume set by a wide group of scholars. Text covers background information and extensive comments on the entire Bible.

Layman's Bible Book Commentary. Nashville: Broadman Press. Twenty-four volumes, written in clear readable style, designed to give a thorough and easily understood exposition of each book of the Bible.

The Daily Study Bible Series by William Barclay. Eighteen volumes on the New Testament. Easy to read with introductory material on each New Testament book plus commentary on the whole New Testament. Westminster Press.

The Interpreter's Bible, edited by George A. Buttrick and others. A twelve-volume set on both the

Old and New Testament. Includes extensive background and explanatory material with commentary and exegesis on the entire Bible. Abingdon-Cokesbury Press.

The One Volume Commentary edited by J. R. Dummelow. A dictionary sized book containing studies on the whole Bible. Macmillan Press.

Peake's Commentary on the Bible, edited by Matthew Black and H. H. Rowley. One volume commentary on the whole Bible. Nelson, Publishers.

Bible Dictionaries:

Miller, Madeleine S. and J. Lane. *Harper's Bible Dictionary*. Harper & Row, 1973. One volume encyclopedia-type book containing information on an extensive range of biblical topics.

Buttrick, George A. and Crim, Keith R. eds. *The Interpreter's Dictionary of the Bible*. Abingdon, 1976. Five volumes that identify and explain all proper names and significant terms and subjects in the Bible, including the Apocrypha. Gives special attention to archaeological discoveries that shed light on the life and faith of ancient biblical times.

Geography and Maps:

The Golden Bible Atlas. A simple illustrated introduction to the lands of the Bible. Golden Press.

Westminster Historical Maps of Bible Lands, edited by G. Ernest Wright and Floyd V. Filson. An excellent study of Bible lands. Westminster Press.

Writings from Biblical Times:

Ancient Near Eastern Texts Relating to the Old Testament, edited by J. B. Pritchard contains excerpts from documents written during the time of the Old Testament. Princeton University Press.

Wars of the Jews and *Antiquities of the Jews*, two writings by Josephus, a Jewish historian of the first century.

Useful Additions:

History books on ancient Near Eastern civilizations can be a great help to the Bible student, as well as general encyclopedias and magazines such as the *National Geographic* which frequently has articles on subjects related to Bible study.